THE

FRAUD

FACTOR

Recognize It.
Overcome It.

Bruce E. Roselle, PhD

Leader Press, Minneapolis, MN

LEADER PRESS is a registered trademark of Roselle Leadership Strategies, Inc., Minneapolis, MN. Communication should be directed to *info@roselleleadership.com*. Visit the website *www.roselleleadership.com* for more information about other publications from LEADER PRESS.

ISBN 13:978–0–9785646–2–9

Library of Congress Catalog Number: 2015921437
Printed in the United States of America

The Fraud Factor is available in ebook and paperback on Amazon.com.

March 2017

Eileen – may this book
help you be even
more authentic!

TABLE OF CONTENTS

ACKNOWLEDGMENTS

No book reaches publication without a great number of people contributing to it in various and important ways. I wish to thank all of them for their input, both critical and supportive. In particular, I wish to thank these folks:

- Numerous coaching clients and workshop participants who, upon hearing the title and main focus of the book, encouraged me to move forward and publish it.
- The many individuals whose stories and struggles with fraud feelings were captured on these pages.
- My monthly CBMC small business owner advisory group, that helped me decide when and how to publish the manuscript. Thanks for your perspective, prayers, and listening ears—Tim Newton, Mike Parker, Mark Stout, Brian Baas, Brian Bohnsack, Thor Smith, Brett Yerks, Joe Field, and Shawn Morrison!
- Jamie Morrison and her crew at Books by the Bundle, who proofread, edited, designed the

cover, and put the manuscript into its final visual format. Great work!

- My daughter, Kate, for her excellent photography on my cover portrait!
- My son, Ben, who listened to my concerns about publishing the book and provided sage advice, and his wife, Erin, who provided additional encouragement.
- My wife of 40 years, Cindy, who was supportive, heartening, and loving throughout the five years of this project. I love you!
- My friend and primary source of strength, peace, and joy in this life, Jesus Christ.

DEDICATION

The Fraud Factor is dedicated to all who have felt like a fraud at some point in their lives and have struggled to work past those feelings. May this book shine a light on the origin and nature of your fraud feelings, and then help you to rediscover your true self.

FOREWORD

For more than 25 years, I have coached and trained thousands of managers and executives to become more effective leaders. In listening to them describe their work and life challenges, I have developed a broad understanding of how they get in their own way, as well gleaned a bit of wisdom and perspective to share with them. The wisdom is not something for which I take credit personally. Rather, I know it is the result of men and women openly sharing their stories and situations with me and their struggles to understand others and respond to them with greater finesse.

The Fraud Factor was initially inspired by several senior executives who had found themselves in a new job situation that suddenly made them doubt their leadership abilities. This resulted in them believing that they needed to be fundamentally different in their new roles, and this belief had undermined their ability to be effective. Though my work since then has focused primarily on organizational leaders, I believe the concepts in this book apply to all of us, not just formally designated leaders.

In the past six years, I have become increasingly aware of the toxic impact of these undermining thoughts and feelings, as well as the many nuances of behavior associated with it. I have begun to recognize that this "fraud factor" is the most common underlying reason that leaders do not succeed.

In many ways, my perspective on this topic began forming in 1988, the year I left a position as a university staff psychologist to join a major psychological consulting firm. I had left the public sector to join the private sector for the first time in my career.

My new career direction felt very different and unfamiliar to me, from getting ready for work in the morning, to working late into the evening. I was accustomed to a university schedule and dress code. Now, for the first time in my life, I wore a suit and tie every day and took on the role of corporate consultant. Unconsciously, as I tied my tie the first several days and put on my dress shoes, I began to believe deep in the core of my being that I needed to become a very different person if I was to be successful in this new, for-profit world.

Imperceptibly on the inside, I started to move away from what had made me successful in my previous jobs, and to move toward a style that seemed to fit this new, foreign environment. As Dorothy observed to Toto in The Wizard of Oz, it was *"not Kansas anymore."* For several months I continued to try to be this new person in a business suit, thinking and hoping that I was fooling everyone around me. I was determined to 'fake it until I make it' in this new work world.

Then, it was my birthday, and the consulting team threw a small party for me and gave me a book as a present. It was *How to Win Friends and Influence People*, by Dale Carnegie. I thought it was a joke, and I laughed along with them. I soon discovered that the situation was not actually funny. Shortly after the birthday party, and well in advance of my midyear review, my boss met with me to give me feedback. I waited anxiously and hopefully for his assessment of my work so far, and he simply said, *"Well, the administrative staff hates working with you."*

Ouch—that was much worse than I had anticipated! I asked for clarification, and he shared with me their impression of how difficult and arrogant I was, and how, thus far, I made no effort to build relationships with them. It was a blunt and raw assessment that threw me off track for several days. I sulked quietly in my office, reflecting on the situation and letting my open wounds heal a bit.

Who am I? As I thought about it, I began to recognize that I had not been myself from the very beginning in this new environment. In fact, since the first day I had not felt that I could be me, and it was not just the suit and tie I had to wear. I had compensated by taking on the new behaviors and attitudes that I thought would lead to success in this new environment. Unfortunately, this led to my drifting far away from my core personality and style. In my fear of not fitting in and getting fired, I was dangerously close to both.

From that moment of clear insight (and a healthy dose of embarrassment), I determined to correct people's perceptions of me by allowing my real personality to show through, letting my style and abilities speak for themselves, and responding to my coworkers and the clients we served more from my heart. I resolved not to try proving anything to my coworkers, but, instead, to just be myself. In support of this new plan, I also scheduled time every day to connect with the administrative staff and actually get to know them and their families on a personal level.

About a month later, shortly before our mid-year reviews were scheduled, my boss pulled me aside and asked me how I thought things were going with the staff and other consultants. I said I was not sure, but I had changed some fundamental behaviors and attitudes, and I hoped they were noticing. He said, *"Well, I don't know what you're doing, but you've totally turned things around. Congratulations... and keep it up!"*

At the time, I did not think of it this way, but I now know that this personal turnaround occurred because I stopped feeling like a fraud in this new environment. Instead, I reconnected to the core of who I was and stopped trying to be the person I thought I needed to be. I felt more relaxed and confident, and it seemed that others began responding with friendlier, more open attitudes toward me.

At bonus time that year, my boss handed me a large check and said, *"Good job—you actually worked out better than I thought you would."* I was not entirely certain what he meant by this comment, but decided to interpret it in the most positive way possible! Then, I quickly cashed the check before he could change his mind.

Feeling like a fraud. Flash forward to a time much more recently, as I began to build the chapters of this book and talk to various people about the main focus. Almost imperceptibly at first, and then much stronger, the thought began to creep into my mind that I was not the best person to handle this fraud topic. Certainly, there must be an author and speaker who had spent more time in this area, who had better stories, and who would be a much more powerful presenter on the topic than me. In short, I began to feel like a fraud about being the one writing and speaking on the topic of being a fraud!

This reaction on my part illustrated to me how pervasive and insidious this fraud feeling can be, and how quickly it can surface. It reminded me how fragile genuineness often is, and how events and circumstances can undermine even the most confident and competent leaders. I began to recognize that many combinations of factors can create situations where leaders begin to feel like, and thus become, frauds in the performance of their jobs, or in their relationships with others.

When I use the word 'fraud,' I mean feeling inauthentic, like a phony or charlatan in a particular situation that, in your mind, requires you to pretend to be someone very different from the person you really are.

In the following chapters, my hope is that you will come to recognize how the fraud factor undermines your success and that of the people you lead. I hope you will see that, while it is important to build new skills and perspectives throughout your life, you will be most effective when you stay true to who you are at the core. In fact, it is impossible to be highly effective if you stray too far from the nucleus of who you are.

Even though I do not know you personally, I believe that the message shared in this book will help you become the powerful, genuine person you truly are inside. With these new insights and strategies, you can get past any thoughts that you might have about being a fraud, and, instead, move confidently into your current roles and future roles. You can do it!

INTRODUCTION

Core Concept: When things change in your role or responsibilities, the new circumstances might generate feelings of inadequacy in you. A lesser degree of these feelings will create dissonance, whereas a greater degree might have the effect of destabilizing you for an extended period of time. Feeling dissonance is a natural outcome of the growth process, but it can become immobilizing if this feeling turns into destabilization, threatening the very core of who you are as a person and as a leader. When you become destabilized, you start to feel like a fraud.

On some level, in certain situations, every leader feels like a fraud. Even the most successful and confident leaders find themselves in settings where they begin to believe that someone else would have been a much better choice to handle their assigned duties. This is often the result of circumstances where they are placed in a new role with very challenging expectations, given unanticipated critical feedback on a 360-degree instrument, or moved under a new manager with a very different approach. Things change, and they suddenly do not feel adequate to the task.

As an executive coach, I see these fraud feelings most frequently in situations where leaders move into a new role with increased scope of responsibility, often over functional areas where they have limited expertise. Sharon is an example of a person in this situation. She came into the department from a parallel position within a business recently acquired by my client company. Though she was put in charge of functions that included her area of technical comfort, she also now had responsibility for several areas about which she knew very little.

Sharon came in wearing heavy spurs and riding hard on the groups for which she was responsible. As she told me later, *"During the interview process, I was informed that major changes needed to be made in the groups I managed. It was clear that their previous boss was too hands-off and lenient, and that a laissez-faire attitude had developed within the teams. A couple of the teams were worse than the others, but they all needed strong leadership."*

Instead of getting to know each person who reported to her and building a team collaboratively, Sharon quickly began to make dramatic changes in the organizational structure, and in the expectations she set for individual members of the teams in her scope of responsibility. This kind of strain on the system would have created a problematic level of stress on the teams all by themselves, but further complicating things with her direct reports, she was displaying inconsistent behavior and occasional emotional outbursts.

When we first met, it became clear to me that Sharon was overwhelmed and anxious in this new role. She made comments to me like, *"I'm not really an expert across all areas of my new responsibility, and the company took a bit of a chance bringing me in."* She also said, *"I think my boss wants to leverage my confidence and strong leader presence to inspire and drive these teams to greater productivity and, ultimately, better success. However, they don't seem too motivated to ratchet-up their game."*

She recognized that her lack of familiarity with several of the functional areas in her scope of responsibilities might create credibility problems for her. Moreover, her new boss had led her to believe that she would be held accountable for quickly turning things around in these areas. On another occasion, for example, she confided in me, *"I've got to show that I am successfully changing the culture in this group, and it has to happen within the first three months."*

Sharon did not want to fail in this new assignment with this new company. Consequently, in critical aspects of this job, she felt that she needed to cover her inadequacies by pushing hard and scoring quick wins. In her own way, she was feeling like a fraud in the position. This led to behaviors that very nearly undermined her success.

Like Sharon, Diane experienced a similar internal reaction when her job changed from supervising others 'putting parts in a box' to managing an entire function. When she had worked the parts job, she could clearly measure her progress and track her success with her team at the end of the day. In her new leadership role, however, the impact of her work was much more intangible. She indicated that for months she had felt like a fraud in her new role.

At first, she felt alone in these emotions and was convinced that her peers did not suffer from feeling like frauds. However, she finally found enough courage one day to mention her feelings of inadequacy to others, and all of them, both male and female peers, indicated that they also had moments where they felt like frauds. Even though she found out that this feeling was shared by others, she kept beating up on herself every day, telling herself; *"You don't know what you're doing—you don't have a clue."* She also lived in fear that her boss would come into her office, shut the door, and say these same words to her, followed by, *"You're fired!"*

After experiencing a high degree of upset for several months in her new supervisory role, Diane began to self-assess the attributes that earned her this role in the first place. She realized that, having started her career in customer service rather than operations, she actually was quite gifted at taking care of people's needs and using her common sense to solve problems. She also recognized that, at several previous places in her career, she had stepped into roles for which she was not fully qualified, and yet had handled them effectively.

In this new role, however, she was given a seat at the senior leadership table. This intimidated her, because she was now sitting across the room from the men and women she had admired, and of whom she stated that she felt *"were way beyond where I was at that point."* They were more highly educated, more experienced, and had longer tenures at the company. Most days, she lived in fear that she would make a wrong decision that would negatively affect other people's lives. Though the intimidation was very strong for her in the first several months, she eventually reconnected with her fundamental attributes that had helped her be successful in her career so far. When she did, she changed and adapted her approach to fit her new role more effectively.

Sharon's and Diane's stories illustrate what happens when individuals feel pushed outside their confidence zone so far that they become off-balance and less than fully effective. To help you better understand the underpinnings of feeling like a fraud, let's discuss some words that may be familiar to you. However, I will use them in a way that might seem new or different.

Dissonance versus destabilization. When things change in your role or responsibilities, there is always the possibility that the new circumstances will generate feelings of inadequacy in you. A lesser degree of these feelings will create a feeling of dissonance, whereas a greater degree might have the effect of destabilizing you for an extended period of time. Allow me to explain the difference more clearly.

Dissonance is a temporary lack of consistency or compatibility between your actions and beliefs in a particular situation. It is a short-term instability that feels unpleasant and motivates you toward resolution.

A temporary **dissonance** brought about by challenging circumstances is usually a healthy road to learning and developing new skills, much like pruning a plant helps spur new growth. In fact, the feeling of dissonance is often the catalyst that spurs on new thinking or ways of approaching people in a different, more effective manner. This was ultimately the case with Sharon and Diane, because their initial fraud feelings began to dissipate as they started talking with their teams, recognizing core characteristics that would help them be successful in the role, and reaching out to peers. They both became effective leaders by developing new approaches and perspectives to help them handle their challenging situations.

By contrast, when people feel a degree of **destabilization** in their core personality, abilities, motivators, and thinking, the fraud factor often appears. The difference is in the degree to which leaders feel pushed outside their confidence zone.

Destabilization is a deep and lasting insta-bility that undermines and overwhelms your ability to function with consistent actions and beliefs. Over time, it disrupts and weakens your capacity to fulfill your roles.

The growth paradox. This dissonance/destabiliza-tion distinction forms the basis for a seeming par-adox as it applies to creating sustainable growth in people like you:

- To **shift your approach** and show evidence of true growth (like Sharon and Diane), you must accommodate to new circumstances and demands by changing some of your core beliefs, which then shifts your behavior; however,
- To **sustain this growth**, you must stay within the boundaries of your core personality, abili-ties, and motivations. Otherwise, the changes will be brief and inauthentic, or you will desta-bilize the core of who you are and awaken the fraud factor.

Sustainable growth. To create sustainable growth, new learning must occur within the context of your existing personality, abilities, motivators, and think-ing—your core. At the same time, true growth seldom occurs unless events or circumstances challenge the basis upon which you think and respond. This is the paradox! You feel dissonance in this kind of situation, and then respond by either finding ways to incorporate new learning, or ignoring the circumstances and continuing in your old paradigm.

However, when you encounter much more dramatic circumstances, you might begin to feel inadequate inside your existing internal framework. Instead of just a bit of dissonance, you may feel a much stronger level of destabilization that threatens to undermine your sense of self. If you do not find new ways to deal with these circumstances, you will start to believe that you really are the fraud you feel you are in the role.

This is a dynamic tension, a learning dance that takes place throughout your life. Feeling dissonance is a natural outcome of the growth process, but it can become immobilizing if this feeling turns into destabilization, threatening the very core of who you are as a person and as a leader. When you become destabilized—feeling upset, losing confidence, or being overwhelmed by the challenges in your environment—you start to feel like a fraud.

The core. I have used the term 'core' several times so far, but have not yet defined it. We will look at this in much greater detail later in the book, but for now, will use the following definition:

> Your core is the essence of who you are as a person—your fundamental nucleus of unique characteristics that are sustained, consistent, and enduring over time. Measurable core characteristics include personality, abilities, motivations, and beliefs/values.

The chapter on Finding the Right Fit, and the three chapters that follow, will help you determine who you are at the core and how to leverage that to become the most effective person you can be. Before those chapters, however, we will look more specifically at what happens when you encounter situations that:

- destabilize you to the core
- convince you that everything you know is wrong, and
- stir up the 'Big Fat Lie' to undermine your effectiveness

Stick with me, now—there are helpful strategies starting in the following chapters! In the following pages, Burt's story illustrates the kinds of situations that lead to destabilization.

QUESTIONS TO CONSIDER AND DISCUSS

➡ When in your career have you felt disso-nance or destabilization as the result of new situations or circumstances? What was your initial reaction?

➡ Have you experienced situations that stretched you outside your comfort zone, creating the "growth paradox" described in this chapter? How did this change over time; did it lead to sustained growth on your part?

EVERYTHING I KNOW SEEMS WRONG!

Core Concept: Being confronted by new information, situations, and perspectives that radically differ from yours, can make it seem that everything you know is suddenly wrong and insufficient to the problems at hand. When you actually develop a deep belief that everything you know IS wrong, it can destabilize you and stir up fraud feelings. And, sometimes, most everything you know is actually inadequate in the situation, and you must change your approach.

Back in the 1970's, a group called Firesign Theater released a humorous album called "Everything you know is wrong!" It was hilariously funny at the time, but, since then, I have encountered a number of situations where most of what I knew WAS wrong. Life sometimes has a way of making funny things serious.

You may have had similar experiences in your life. As we discussed in the last chapter, being confronted by new information, situations, and perspectives that radically differ from your prior understanding of how things work, can make it seem that everything you know is suddenly wrong and insufficient to the problems at hand. This type of situation nearly always generates some dissonance as you try to make sense of things and decide how to respond. However, when you actually develop a deep belief that everything you know IS wrong, it can destabilize you and stir up fraud feelings.

Such was the case with Burt, a 40-something clinical researcher who had been enjoying his role as the team lead, until suddenly a new boss stepped onto the scene. It felt abrupt because Burt thought that he would continue to lead the clinical trials team. However, senior management decided to create a new level of leadership to which Burt and the rest of the clinical team would report. Burt was not considered as a candidate for this new role. In a sense, Burt had received his first demotion in nearly 10 years of work at this company, and in almost 20 years in the diabetes medical device industry. His reaction to the new circumstances was to feel destabilized and overwhelmed, and to employ a hide and avoid strategy.

His new boss, Yolanda, was at least 10 years younger than Burt, and had moved quickly up the ranks in her previous company. Lured away to take on this new role, she was smart, well educated, and personable. However, she and Burt got off to a poor start when, in her mind, the dynamics between them were more competitive than collaborative. Based on the information she had been given by Burt's previous boss, as well as her early observations of him, she did not see any evidence of him functioning appropriately as a leader in this organization. He seemed to be in denial and unable to step into his new, lesser functional leadership role.

This represented a sort of 'one-two' punch for Burt. The first blow occurred when he was not considered for the newly created leadership position. The second happened when his new boss viewed him as incompetent and difficult. Burt felt like a fraud in his new role, because he believed that Yolanda wanted him to be someone totally different from who he had been up to this point in his career.

Burt described his early interactions with Yolanda by saying, *"We haven't even talked much in one-on-one meetings, but she already feels antagonistic to me. She expects me to keep her informed down to the tiniest level of detail, and, if she discovers something I did not tell her—usually because I thought it was too trivial—she becomes accusatory and upset."*

Since Burt had been in the lead role before Yolanda arrived, he continued to receive emails and voice-mails from people around the company asking for his expert perspective weeks after his boss had started. In response, he simply answered many of their questions and weighed in on problems without thinking that he was overstepping the boundaries of his boss's new role. He explained that, *"Others don't know her well enough to have confidence in her in the role, so they come to me as they have in the past. I'm trying not to overwhelm her with decisions that I should be making at my level, but she thinks I'm being secretive. She clearly does not trust me, and, frankly, I don't trust her, either."*

Part of the problem was that he, in fact, was not certain what responsibilities his new role and the boss's role now included. In the absence of specifics about his new job description, he saw his role as simply filling in the blanks and protecting Yolanda's backside from potential problems. He tried to step in and deflect the impact of some of the early decisions she made, but she interpreted his actions as resistance, not protection.

Because he had always been certain of the scope of his job and what was expected of him in the past, not knowing these things created a destabilized tailspin in him. The harder he tried to figure out who Yolanda wanted him to be, the closer he came to crashing. His reaction to this was to stay in his office and dig into details that, unfortunately, were not priorities to his boss.

Yolanda had come into the organization determined to right the ship and make some quick changes that would be viewed by her manager as early wins. Specifically regarding Burt, she indicated, *"He wanted the job I was hired to do, but he was not even considered for the role. However, he seems to be doggedly hanging on to the idea that others made a mistake in not choosing him. Consequently, he weighs in on topics and makes decisions as if he was the top person, and he fails to keep me adequately informed. It feels like he's hiding something, waiting for me to step into a trap so he can say 'gotcha' to me."*

In Burt's opinion, Yolanda headed off half-cocked and ill-advised right out of the blocks in the decisions she was making. After about two months of this awkward dance between Burt and Yolanda, Tony from Human Resources contacted me about the possibility of providing coaching for Burt. The goal was to help him stop mourning the old role and begin embracing the new one. More important in some ways, my objective was to bring Burt to the point where he accepted Yolanda as his new boss and found ways to make her successful. To do that, I needed to help him stabilize, move away from the fraudulent behaviors he had adopted, and become re-grounded in his core as a leader.

After several meetings with Yolanda, Burt, and Tony, I thought I had figured out the major dynamics in the picture. My clear understanding from Yolanda was that Burt needed to get on board the new train, or have his car de-coupled somewhere on a side rail. Sensing that I did not have much time to turn this around, I began to work with Burt immediately. He was as a 'deer in the headlights' when we first began talking, still trying to understand how he had ended up in this smaller role, and highly suspect of what my function would be as his coach in 'fixing' him. His face reflected the perplexed look of 'everything I know seems wrong' in the new situation, and he was clueless as to how to maneuver from there.

Once Burt and I established an understanding of how we would work together, we discussed more deeply how he saw his situation and what strategies he had employed so far to create success in the new role. The more he revealed to me, the clearer it became that, while Burt was understandably resistant about this new situation into which he had been thrust without input, he was also approaching the new circumstances with the same tools and perspective that he had used in the old role. In fact, he was using the same tools and perspective that he had used for most of the last 20 years of his career. I decided that it was time to help him see that, in some ways, everything he knew WAS wrong.

We started with 360-degree feedback and personality tests that I interpreted for him. The picture from these data was quite clear. I helped summarize the results for him by saying, *"Burt, the good news is that you are viewed as a technologically savvy scientist who is steady and predictable emotionally, assertive in your communication, and empathetic in your relationships. The bad news is that you are not viewed as a strong team player, nor as someone who can inspire others or generate enthusiasm, and you tend to be a bottleneck for work the team is trying to complete on time. They see you as a strong, logical and analytical thinker who does not have a real commitment to urgency."*

My blunt assessment of these 360-degree data surprised Burt, and he became red-faced and defensive about the comments and ratings. He was having a hard time assimilating them into his view of himself as a leader; consequently, he could only dismiss or debate them. He was obviously flummoxed about the perspective others provided to describe him, and this seemed to stir up even more fear about being a fraud.

As a coach, my strategy and approach with him was very different than with Sharon and Diane in the previous chapter. Over the course of our in-person meetings, as well as phone calls or emails between sessions, I deliberately supported the validity of the data that brought stark reality to his concept of himself as a leader, while at the same time, affirming the value of who he was at the core as a person. The 'core' data we used came from his strengths on the 360-degree feedback, his personality test results, and his self-assessment of his primary motivators at work. This was a delicate dance with Burt, but I knew the organization wanted very much to retain him in his key technical role and they wanted him to be happy.

On the continuum from dissonance to destabilization, Sharon and Diane were on the temporary dissonance end. Their new circumstances had forced them to shift their approaches in order to grow and be successful. However, they did not doubt themselves in their core attributes as leaders. Burt, on the other end of the continuum, experienced a deep and lasting instability that pushed him off his foundation.

In later chapters we will discuss further the approach I took with Burt, to help him move out of destabilization. This discussion will help you work your own way through situations that have caused similar reactions in you. But first, we will look at how, in Burt's case and in many other situations, feeling like a fraud and developing fraudulent behaviors can potentially lead to losing your job.

QUESTIONS TO CONSIDER AND DISCUSS

➡ In your career, have you ever experienced a time when, like Burt, it seemed like everything you knew was wrong? What led to this feeling and how did you respond to it?

➡ As a leader, what strategies and techniques have you employed to shift the approach of a direct report who responded with resistance and defensiveness to changes you made?

FRAUDS GET FIRED

Core Concept: When you feel like most everything you know is not adequate to your situation, you might begin to engage in fraudulent behaviors. These are things you do to cover your fear and confusion, and to try to be what you believe others want you to be. In these situations, you must let go of the fraudulent behaviors and shift to an approach that helps you grow into the new circumstances, and that reflects your genuine, true self. Otherwise, you run the risk of getting fired!

My purpose in the approach I took with Burt in the previous chapter was to work the paradox identified in the Introduction to this book. That is, to leverage the knowledge that a degree of dissonance is necessary to create any growth. Burt clearly needed to exhibit growth as a leader. The goal was to dramatically shift his fundamental beliefs about how he came across to others, and what he needed to do to be effective in his role.

At the same time, ironically, I intentionally underscored and affirmed who Burt was at the core, repeating my commitment that we would do nothing to try to change his fundamental personality, motivations, or strengths. The ultimate goal was to help him accept who he was and who he was not, and to embrace his narrower technical role. We needed to help him let go of the fraudulent behaviors he had adopted and shift to an approach that reflected his genuine self.

What is meant by his **fraudulent behaviors**? Those things that Burt did to cover his fear and confusion, and to try to be what he thought Yolanda wanted him to be. For most people, these kinds of behaviors are awkward and ill-fitting, and, like with Burt, they are typically carried out in an ineffective manner. Yolanda was not asking him to be a different person at the core; rather, she simply wanted him to approach situations with a different leader mindset. The new approach he needed to embrace as his own required him to become a collaborator who uses an influencing style, rather than an orchestrator who directs others' work, and to take full responsibility for his area of clinical expertise.

Burt's story illustrates that human beings generally have a high need for equilibrium in their work and lives, and anything that undermines or rattles this is typically perceived as a threat. Progress in our coaching relationship was slow and painful at times, with Burt successfully navigating through some of the turbulence of having to accommodate to the new role and its changed expectations. However, these were minor wins to his boss, who was still fundamentally frustrated with Burt's inability to make the needed shift.

Regrettably, the destabilization he experienced at the beginning of the circumstances, which included a new manager and altered role, kept Burt from developing into the leader he needed to become. After about a year of our coaching work, he was put on a performance improvement plan by Yolanda. Six months later, his employment was terminated. He never understood fully how much needless time and effort he had spent covering his fears, engaging in self-protective behaviors, and failing to make the necessary changes in his approach.

From my coaching experience with Burt, I began to see that frauds get fired. Leaders who become destabilized through new, challenging experiences, and who then compensate for this by developing a set of ineffective, fear-based behaviors, inadvertently set up a situation in which their employment might well be terminated. More often than not, they do get fired.

Another employee, Salim, represents a variation on the theme of fraudulent behaviors; unfortunately, behaviors that ultimately led to his dismissal. He was a senior executive who, from a major retailer's corporate headquarters, oversaw every retail facility. We had begun to work together in a coaching relationship because his interpersonal skills were viewed as deficient, and he tended to leave bodies in his wake as he made decisions and moved into action.

As in my typical coaching engagements, we gathered some 360-degree feedback information from direct reports and peers, as well as his manager. The feedback from most respondents was a bit 'vanilla', but we were able to cobble together a picture of his relative strengths and development areas. We started working on developing insight about what drove his unproductive interpersonal behaviors, and how to replace them with more effective ones.

Though we had completed several coaching sessions, I developed the nagging feeling that he was saying what he thought I wanted to hear, but not working on new approaches between our meetings. I was concerned that he was not actually changing his behavior with his team. Several times, I requested a time when I could observe him in staff interactions, so that I could judge for myself. Each time, however, he came up with a reason why the meetings had to be rescheduled to a later date. He also seemed uncomfortable in our coaching sessions, like he just wanted them to be done so he could check another one off his list.

About half-way through our coaching sessions, his company sent out an organization-wide employee survey. His team members filled it out, and, unlike their earlier 360-degree coaching feedback, they were very critical of Salim. They indicated that he was a dictator with them, threatening reprisal if they did not comply and not listening when they tried to engage him in conversation about an issue. Their scores on him were so low, in fact, that senior management decided to fire him shortly after the results came out.

One of the reasons they fired him at once is that they were afraid he would engage in reprisals with his team members. In fact, as I looked more closely at his 360-degree results from the start of our coaching, I saw a pattern of moderate ratings and either no comments or evasive comments from his team. Apparently, his team had felt unsafe when asked to supply this earlier feedback, but had felt more protected for the broad-based employee survey.

Before Salim had been promoted into his executive role, he had not exhibited the behaviors identified in his employee survey feedback. He had been viewed as someone who was direct and had high standards for his team, and he had the reputation for being responsible to make sure tasks were done at the utmost level of quality. However, due to his fears of being viewed as a fraud in this new role, he took on new behaviors and exaggerated old ones to the point that he was let go. He became a tyrant about quality, holding his team personally responsible for any slip. Further, he became punitive and vindictive, threatening team members with their jobs if they complained about him. In his attempt to cover his fears that he did not belong in his executive role and might fail in it, he tried to protect himself with new 'executive' behaviors. These led to his downfall. Frauds get fired.

Fortunately, in some cases, it is possible to save a situation that seems headed for termination. This was the case with Kay.

She had left a company where she had worked in a senior financial consulting role for nearly 15 years, and then joined a competing firm. During the interview process, her future boss and peers were impressed with her direct, thoughtful style and her confident eagerness to guide her potential new team into new revenue streams. They felt that her style would work well in the existing culture, and that her ideas would help raise the bar on her team to the next level of excellence.

However, Kay had made the mistake of talking with a number of colleagues and former bosses before she took on this new role. They had filled her with fears about getting fired if she did not score some dramatic wins in the first 90 days of her tenure. As a result, she abandoned her initial plan of getting to know her team's strengths and areas of development, through one-on-one meetings. She set aside her thoughts of collaborating with them to see what was working well and what they felt needed to change, before she came to any conclusions.

Instead, she vacillated between making abrupt changes and hiding in her office. On more than one occasion, she was heard to say, *"When I was with my former company, we did things this way, and we were very successful,"* and *"You brought me in because I am the expert, so listen to me!"* Kay came across as defensive and blunt whenever she faced opposition. At other times, she avoided contact with her team by working alone in her office, or traveling to a client site.

Things reached a tipping point when, after six months, her new boss sat down with her and asked pointedly; *"What happened to the person we met in the interviews and decided to hire?"* Her boss indicated that Kay needed to turn perceptions around quickly, or her continued employment would be in jeopardy. Frauds get fired.

The good news for Kay was that, while the stress of the new role had destabilized her, it had not fully undermined her. She still had enough perspective to recognize that she needed to reach out to others and figure out how to mend fences and create a fresh start. Because we had worked together in a previous coaching relationship, she contacted me to help her work through this new situation. After a great deal of hard work on her part, and more than a few apologies, she eventually turned things around.

Frauds get fired, yes, but only if they have become fully destabilized and have developed fraudulent behaviors that are quite ineffective. When leaders like Burt, Kay, and Salim lack insight about how problematic their fraud feelings and fraudulent behaviors have become, they typically undermine their effectiveness to such a degree that it is impossible to fix things. If your current situation has destabilized you, it is not too late to reverse the negative perceptions. Start by learning in the next chapter how a 'Big, Fat Lie' might be undermining your confidence.

QUESTIONS TO CONSIDER AND DISCUSS

➡ Have you ever been in danger of being fired, or feared for your job security, as a result of feeling destabilized in the role? What did you do to turn things around?

➡ Have you been in situations where co-workers, or a boss, was fired for some of the behaviors discussed in this chapter? What specific ineffective actions did they engage in that led to their termination?

THE BIG FAT LIE

Core Concept: The Big Fat Lie is simply the belief that you are not adequate in the situation or circumstances you currently face. Most people suffer from some variation of this lie. Believing the lie somehow gives you the crutch or the rationalization for why you are not as successful as you had hoped, or others had expected you to be. Sometimes, the lie is not very powerful; other times, it feels overwhelming, like a jagged mountain or a cavernous hole. The problem is that the lie, while it seems to explain things on some level, also acts in a self-fulfilling way to inhibit your optimal effectiveness.

urt's reaction to his work situation in Chapter 2 illustrates what can happen when leaders experience a sense of destabilization in their work and are pushed outside their comfortable boundaries by circumstances they experience. The question you might be asking right now is, *"What precipitates the feelings of destabilization in people like Burt?"* The answer is: the ugly appearance of the Big Fat Lie.

In Burt's case, the lie he believed and shared with me was, *"People don't really understand me, and there's no one here to protect me, other than me."* He had told himself this lie as a young child, and he continued to operate as if it were true. This forced him to distrust people and continuously question their motives. It also pushed him to always be in control, to never admit a mistake, and to defend himself and explain his actions whenever possible.

In general, what is the **Big Fat Lie**? It is simply the belief that you are not adequate in the situation or circumstances you face. As we discussed previously, this often occurs when you face new, unfamiliar challenges that make you begin to doubt your ability to handle them. When the changed circumstances seem extremely challenging to you, and, like Burt, you feel overwhelmed and paralyzed, you might begin to think that everything you know is wrong and you are totally inadequate to the task. You might start to doubt yourself and your abilities. You might even experience a level of destabilization at the core of your being, like Burt did. When the lie is not quite so big and fat, you might experience, instead, the less overwhelming feelings of dissonance.

In David's case, for example, he experienced dissonance in his new role. When David and his manager first met with me to talk about starting a coaching relationship, several factors were clear immediately. David was an extremely bright VP who had grown up in the finance part of the high-tech manufacturing company in which he was employed. He was personable in an introverted sort of way, displaying an easy smile and a wry, somewhat random, sense of humor.

Having spent a number of years in the industry, as an accountant and then controller, David had shifted to a business development role after having completed an MBA. Within the previous year, he had been promoted to a product line management role in which he was responsible for more than two billion dollars of revenue. Shortly after having been promoted to this role, his manager called me in to meet with him and start an executive coaching engagement.

In the first meeting with David and his manager, she described him as, *"someone who struggles a bit taking a strong, definitive stand in the midst of uncertainty. That is, he often seems uncomfortable going with a hunch when he doesn't have what he feels is a sufficient amount of data to support his conclusions."* His manager indicated that the most important challenge in David's new role was for him to influence leaders more broadly within the organization, to create the right vision and plan so that others would follow, and to empower his team to make decisions and take action. *"He needs to step up and move to the next level in his leadership, where he thinks about issues across the company and inspires his team to take on new challenges,"* she added.

David's manager also depicted him as often being 'too honest' with others, adding, *"He feels like he must explain all possible financial scenarios that could develop, rather than thinking about and focusing on the courses of action that might be more politically appropriate than others."* From her perspective, he needed to move more quickly to explain the core of the issues and help frame the discussion so that others could get up to speed and on board with his thinking.

For his part, David admitted that he tended to not ask for help until he was in deep water, stating that he believed that he could "*just work my way out of it*." He described himself as, "*the kind of person who stubbornly refuses to admit defeat*," and who, instead, would "*crank up my hard work ethic and put in more hours until I get the job done*." This behavior tended to push his team away when they could have been of the most help, and it took time away from his more important role of influencing the thinking of internal and external customers.

It also contributed to his feelings of being a fraud, because he thought, "*If I'm smart enough to be in this role, I should be able to figure out the answers without needing someone to step in and save me.*" Because he could not always figure out a way to work through a problem he faced, he began to feel inadequate as a leader.

David completed a 360-degree feedback inventory to see how his peers and direct reports would describe his strengths and development areas. From those results, it was clear that others saw him as strong at pushing to achieve high quality results, understanding technology, and communicating in a confident, direct manner. They also saw him as very effective at opening up communication, being genuinely curious about others' thoughts and feelings, and nurturing development in others. They described him as smart, empathetic, and humble.

In areas that others identified as development needs, they wanted him to lead more strategically, with a clearer long-range vision and stronger sense of the business imperatives that would drive future change. They wanted him to manage others more effectively by sharing information more openly, delegating more consistently, and doing more to build consensus. His direct reports urged him to, *"replace micro-management with true empowerment,"* and to, *"listen to others before assuming you have the right answer."* Comments from his peers indicated that they wanted him to, *"develop his long range vision and communicate it,"* as well as to, *"drive change in the cross-functional internal teams."*

Senior management in the organization was keen to support David in his new role. They viewed him as having all the right stuff to be promoted even further, yet needing to change some fundamental ways in which he operated, as reflected in the feedback he received from his manager and his 360-degree results. After reading this feedback and perspective from others, and recognizing that he was not as successful with internal and external customers as he expected himself to be, David wondered whether, in fact, he was the right fit for his new role and responsibilities.

Identifying the lie. David and I had met a couple of times in our coaching engagement before he was comfortable enough to confide in me that he felt like a fraud in his role. He did so by sharing his version of The Big Fat Lie, *"I need to be someone totally different to really be successful in this role."* His peer, Faye, was in a similar product management role, and David began to believe that he needed to fashion his approach to match Faye's personality and style.

As David described it, *"Faye comes from a marketing and sales background, so her personality is naturally much more outgoing and verbal, and way more engaging with customers than mine. She's also extremely confident interacting with internal and external customers, with much greater finesse at casting a vision and enrolling them through her charisma."* David had tried to emulate Faye, but felt like he had failed miserably. This just underscored in his mind that he was a fraud in the role.

I still remember the pained look in David's eyes as he described how much better suited his peer was to their business development role, and how much David felt out of Faye's league. *"She's exactly the kind of person we need in this sort of role; she's very different from me."* As I listened to him, I recognized that, in order to help him take a stand and become highly successful in his new role, he desperately needed an alternative perspective. For a moment, I felt hobbled in my capacity to give him the kind of insightful and uplifting response he required right then. What wisdom could I impart that would turn his defeated attitude around and move him in the right direction?

Then it came to me, and I felt a rush of excitement at the words that formed in my brain! *"No, David,"* I said excitedly, *"You can't be like Faye in your approach, because that would be like trying to wear her clothes or walk in her shoes. You are not Faye, but you are uniquely you. The problem is that you have persuaded yourself that you are a fraud in this role, because your style is so different from Faye's. You have convinced yourself that you are not cut out for this job, even though you are already successful at it*!"

Despite the fact that he was chosen for the role and had been fulfilling it with relative success for nearly two years, David had somehow still harbored the lie that he was not fit to be in the role. Consequently, everything he saw about himself in the role was filtered through this Big Fat Lie, and he continually felt like a fraud, particularly when he was with clients and potential clients.

Feeling like I was gaining momentum now, I went on to say; *"You must do your job from your core, tapping into your unique, signature traits and characteristics, and leveraging them. If you do, you will be the most successful you can be in this role, as well as any future roles you may fill.*" I looked at him to see if he understood, and David had that soft look in his eye that people get when they hear truth spoken to them. Being the fact-based, practical guy he was, he then, of course, asked, "*How do I do that?*" For the moment, I just smiled, knowing that my words had hit home.

This initial conversation led to many others as David and I fleshed out what his core personality characteristics, abilities, motivations, and beliefs were, and strategized how to leverage these fundamental characteristics to maximize his effectiveness. We discovered together that he tends to be most comfortable in a role when he can act as a 'guide' or 'helper' to the people around him.

I challenged him to think of ways he could shift his approach in his current role so that he could function primarily as a guide or helper with his team and customers. We discussed how, in past financial roles, he typically used facts and technical information in his interactions with others to help educate them and respond to their questions. Again, I challenged him by asking, "*Why can't you use a similar style with your internal and external customers, making sure you tailor the amount of data you share to fit their individual needs?"*

The following week, David used this new approach with a group at the headquarters of one of his customers. He thought of himself as an educator/guide who must ask questions to determine the amount of information and perspective they needed, and then respond with an appropriate amount of detail in his responses. After trying out this new approach, he excitedly reported that he had felt confident and relaxed talking with the group, and they had responded very positively to his new strategy. He had not felt like he needed to be a fraud with them, and he dropped the fraudulent behaviors he had previously adopted. It was, in his opinion, the best response he had received from a customer group so far, and he felt encouraged to continue to approach customers from his core style.

Within David, the dissonance was strong and his Big Fat Lie was convincing, but he continued to function at an acceptably high level of effectiveness. He experienced the short-term sense of instability that accompanies dissonance, but he used the coaching and interactions with his customers to nurture a new, deeper sense of confidence in what he brought to the table. He reconnected with his core personality, abilities, motivators, and values, and leveraged them to become even more successful in his role.

His situation had not destabilized him to the degree that Burt's or Salim's had. Why might that be true? Some people are more fragile at the core. Their early family dynamics, as well as their life experiences since then, have made them guarded, defensive, and fearful. They are often less capable of working through conflict, less confident asserting their perspective, and less resilient when things change unexpectedly.

Counteracting the Lie. Since my initial work with David, in working with other leaders I began to see that most of my clients suffer from some variation of The Big Fat Lie. Believing the lie somehow gives them the crutch or the rationalization for why they are not as successful as they had hoped, or others expected them to be. Sometimes, the lie is not very powerful; other times, it feels overwhelming to them, like a jagged mountain or a cavernous hole.

The problem is that the lie, while it seems to explain things on some level, also acts in a self-fulfilling way to inhibit people's effectiveness. The misperception that they must act differently than who they are at the core in order to be successful in their roles undermines their capacity to be highly effective. For some leaders, like Burt and Salim in the previous chapter, it leads to a crushing sense of destabilization, but for others, like David, this creates only a temporary dissonance.

For example, Kate verbalized that her Big Fat Lie was, *"Others will not find me to be acceptable if I fully express myself to them."* Once she realized the negative impact the lie was having on her work and relationships, she was able to focus on what she had to offer. She described the process of deliberately leading from her core as, *"finding my adult voice."* She noted, *"As I become more effective at responding authentically to my team and getting out of my own way as a leader, my team members also feel more confident about expressing themselves in a genuine, real way."* By getting out of her own way and connecting to her core attributes, she also got out of their way.

After Kate and I had been working together for several months, we met with her manager. He described her as *"having developed a higher level of confidence and an increased ability to influence others and partner with her direct reports. At the same time,"* he said, *"I can see that Kate is willing to be more vulnerable, asking for help when she needs it, and adding greater value to others' work by building on it collaboratively."* He recognized that she was becoming more effective at leveraging her own strengths, creating a greater sense of ownership on her team, and leading more fluidly. In short, he viewed her now as a more genuine, grounded leader. From my perspective as her coach, I saw her as someone who was temporarily destabilized by her Big Fat Lie, but who had found a path back to genuineness.

A further example is that of Sam, who met with me for the first time a few weeks after he had received some devastating feedback from his new manager. Sam's previous manager had been very hands-off, in part because that was her style, and, in part, because she did not understand much about his area of expertise in web pages and social networks. Consequently, Sam had simply forged ahead, making independent decisions and receiving no feedback or direction. As he said, "*I never ask my bosses for feedback or direction, because I don't want to burden them by continually reaching out for help. They've got plenty on their plate, already.*" This conclusion turned out to be a problem for Sam and his manager.

His new boss, Eva, sat down with him early on in their working relationship and began peppering Sam with pointed questions about his vision, his plan, and how he spent his time. The more questions Eva posed, the more emotional Sam became until he was angry and defensive. The thing most important to him in his work was to not disappoint others, especially his boss, and he had managed to do that in one awful conversation!

Following this meeting with Sam, Eva met with the VP of Human Resources and others internally. Their conclusion was that Sam should be demoted to a lesser leadership role, because the requirements of that role focused more on following direction and implementing plans, rather than generating the vision and strategy for the department. The senior leaders did not see him as confident enough to fill the role in the way it needed to be carried out. Eva explained to me, *"He does a great job of managing projects and he's also quite personable, but he does not inspire others or bring new ideas to the table as a leader. Unfortunately, that's what we need in his role."*

To his credit, Sam spent only a few hours pitying himself and blaming Eva and his former boss. Then, he cooled down, pulled himself upright, and started to write a strategic plan to lead in the way he now understood the organization needed him to lead. His boss was so impressed with his resilience and the merits of the plan that she changed her mind and decided to keep him in the role. However, she strongly suggested that he work with an executive coach to help keep him on track. That is when Human Resources contacted me about working with Sam.

In our first conversation, we talked about how he had begun to question his own abilities and confidence after his first meeting with Eva. For him, the Big Fat Lie was focused on how his true personality was not acceptable, so he thought, "I need to cover who I am with a very different style." He recognized that, because of the lack of direction from his old boss and his own hesitation to reach out for help and feedback, he had gradually gone off on a trajectory that had not adequately met the organization's needs. He had been like a frog slowly boiling in hot water, unaware of the danger the situation posed to his current effectiveness and the future of his career. The dissonance between who he is, and what he thought his job required him to be, made him feel and act in a fraudulent manner.

As I talked further with Sam, it became clearer that his near-demotion stemmed from more than his failure to check in for feedback and direction. It was also the result of him having increasingly shifted his style and approach over the seven years since he was originally hired into the organization. He told me, *"My more informal style and offbeat sense of humor just seemed to confuse people early on in my career, so I decided I needed to change pretty dramatically. In response to this reaction I got from others, I started to become someone very different at work than the guy my friends and* family know me to be."

By the time his new boss, Eva, came on the scene, he had shifted so far from the center of who he really was that he had become increasingly less confident and more focused on putting out fires and handling daily issues. When Eva had questioned him about the strategy and big picture vision in their first meeting together, he had already lost a significant amount of confidence, and his humor had become brittle and annoying. He felt like a fraud in the role, and others had become confused about his ability to adequately fulfill the requirements of the position.

From these conversations with David, Kate, Sam, and many other coaching clients in the past several years, it became very clear to me how important it is to recognize how the Big Fat Lie undermines one's effectiveness, and then to consciously decide to lead from the core. In fact, being undermined by a lie, feeling like a fraud, and trying to lead from someplace other than one's core attributes, is the primary reason leaders derail. Attempting to lead others with an approach that is not grounded on who one really is at the center of his or her being is a guaranteed recipe for failure. Finding the right fit is also critically important, as we will discuss in the next chapter.

The Fraud Continuum. Burt's situation in the first chapter and his ineffective reaction to it illustrates one end of a continuum related to **The Fraud**

Factor—those individuals who are self-deceived and in denial to a degree about their true capabilities and results. These are the ones that others view as a fraud in a leadership or other work role, because they do not seem to have an accurate picture of their own attributes and limitations.

On the other end of the continuum are those highly successful people who, despite their phenomenal results, see themselves as just one misstep away from failure. Like David in this chapter, these individuals feel like they must hide who they really are and become someone different in order to be successful.

The range of behaviors looks like this:

Inflated Self	Genuine Self	Deflated Self
Holds unrealistically positive self-beliefs	Presents self authentically	Not highly confident
Minimizes critical feedback	Knows self at the core	Sensitive to feedback
Blames others for problems	Confidently handles dissonance	Hyper-critical of self
Deceived about own talents	Open to feedback	Hides true self
Seen by others as a fraud	Realistic about own talents	Anxious about failure
Denies negative feedback		Covers feelings of inadequacy
Inflates own results		Becomes destabilized

Looking at this chart, it is clear that there are major downsides to lack of genuineness as a leader. On the Inflated Self end, there are unrealistic self-beliefs coupled with being viewed as a fraud by others. On the Deflated Self end of the continuum, there are hyper-critical behaviors and failure anxiety.

QUESTIONS TO CONSIDER AND DISCUSS

➥ In this chapter David had a tendency to just put his head down and try to work his way out of things, without thinking about how he could involve others in the solution. To what extent is this similar to or different from your own style? What similarities did you see in the brief stories about Sam, Kate, and others?

➥ What is the Big, Fat Lie that sometimes gets in the way of your success at work? To what extent do you feel successful in your work? How do other key employees view your level of success?

➥ Have you ever tried, like David or Kate or Sam, to change who you are to better fit the requirements of a job? As you look back on it, how well did that work?

➥ Where do you fit on the Fraud Continuum? Which behaviors from all three categories are most typical for you?

FINDING THE RIGHT FIT

Core Concept: Changing who you are at the core is never the best way to handle a set of circumstances in your work. The best strategy is almost always to figure out who you are at the core as a person, and then lead confidently from that genuine foundation. At some point, this approach might lead you to a decision to find a better fit in a different organization or department, but this is not a conclusion you should jump to right away. The goal is to make sure you are functioning at your optimal level, stretching and growing, but still operating within your sweet spot of effectiveness.

Why do organizational leaders think they must lead as someone other than who they really are? What causes people to doubt their capacity to fit into a role, even when the job requirements are not that different from roles they have successfully filled in the past? In the brief vignettes of David, Kate, and Sam, from the last chapter, we have some clues.

Some, like David, start a new position and convince themselves that it is not the right fit. They assume—falsely—that they must approach things very differently than they have in past positions, in order to be successful. Others, like Kate, have deeply-rooted, fear-based doubts about themselves and lack of self-assurance at the core. Consequently, they struggle when they must 'be the adult', as Kate would say, and they unwittingly undermine their ability to lead others confidently. In these situations, any role that requires them to step it up a bit will feel like the wrong fit.

Still others, like Sam, get the strong message from their manager or other senior leaders that they have doubts about their fit with their current role. Consequently, they start to believe that they must function in a completely dissimilar way in order to be successful in the new situation.

In my 30 years of coaching experience, I have never seen a set of circumstances where the best solution to a poor job fit was to attempt to change who an individual is at their core. For emphasis, let me say that again in a slightly different way. Changing who you are at the core is never the best way to handle a set of circumstances or personalities in your work. The best strategy is almost always to figure out who you are as a person, and then work confidently from that genuine foundation. At some point, this approach might lead you to a decision to find a better fit, but this is not a conclusion you should jump to right away.

When I encounter situations where an individual is viewed as a poor fit in a particular position, senior management usually considers terminating or demoting them. If this has been a problem that has not been addressed by previous managers for a number of years, then taking him or her out of the role might be the best solution. Because it is an expensive conclusion that might involve paying severance and conducting a search for another person to fill the vacated role, it should not be reached lightly. However, the emotional and financial costs of keeping someone in a role in which he or she cannot succeed are even more painful.

To illustrate, Jerry was the VP of Sales and Marketing for a medium-sized manufacturing company, and I was called in to work with him by his boss, the CEO. The CEO had hired Jerry to add a level of energy and professionalism to the sales function and to build market share, but Jerry had spent the major portion of his first year in the role putting out fires and learning about the products made by multiple divisions in the company. When he had tried on a few occasions to make a deal with a customer or expand an existing product line, he had managed to upset his peers. The CEO wanted it to work out with Jerry, so he brought me in as a coach; however, he was ambivalent about whether Jerry could be successful in the position.

I started the coaching engagement by conducting phone interviews of 10 key internal customers and peers to gather information on what they perceived as Jerry's strengths and development areas. On the strengths side, they saw him as bright and highly professional, and a strong customer advocate who enthusiastically handled tough issues and worked toward fair solutions. However, they also accused him of going around them or stepping on their toes as he ran with an idea to solve a customer problem. He was viewed as too direct and even arrogant at times, as well as moody and somewhat sarcastic in his sense of humor. They also observed that he was a poor listener who often walked away from an internal meeting with a totally different conclusion than the rest of the participants had reached.

In our first couple of coaching sessions, I recognized that Jerry was, at the core, a strong and confident leader. The psychological tests he took confirmed my interview impressions that he had a great deal to offer to this company. He was trying to lead from his core personality and abilities, but the structure of his position, the poor communication about what his role was to be (it was a new role for the organization), and major issues in his personal life were derailing him.

The approach taken with Jerry was, first, to highlight the strengths he had at the core of his personality and abilities, and then to encourage him to lead from that place. At the same time, we identified underlying irrational fears and faulty beliefs that were the source of the arrogance, moodiness, and lack of team play that his internal customers and peers had described to me in the phone interviews.

Once we worked through the origin and circumstances surrounding his reactive behaviors, he was able to start to turn perceptions around internally and lead from his core. Unfortunately, the changes were too little and too late for the CEO and Jerry's peers, and the decision was made that Jerry was simply not a good fit for what the organization needed from the position. (For a complete understanding of how fears, faulty beliefs, and anchor lies undermine your capacity as a leader, see my 2006 book, **Fearless Leadership**).

As we introduced earlier in the book, in order to create new growth, you must experience situations, perspectives, and circumstances that challenge you, rattle your core, and perhaps require a bit of reorganization of your internal beliefs and approaches. Often, your growth as a person requires you to seek out new experiences, take on new responsibilities, get involved in cross-functional task forces, or learn new information and perspective. Early on in these kinds of assignments that stretch you, it may not seem like the right fit at all. You might convince yourself that you can never be successful in the existing circumstances, and that your only choice is to quit.

Even though you might feel this way, the best outcome in such a situation can sometimes be to stay and make it the right fit through your own growth and development. If your current situation seems like a major stretch, make sure you give it a full, unafraid effort before you throw in the towel. You can do it! As we discussed in the introduction, these situations can birth life changing growth that will force you to adapt your approach to one that is more effective.

However, to sustain such growth and make sure that the roots of your new perspective go deep, the internal reorganization you experience must remain consistent with the essence of who you are. If the new growth and perspective is too overwhelming, and, consequently, undermines your confidence in your fundamental attributes, the resulting destabilization you feel can unleash a long-term version of the fraud factor.

The right fit, then, is one that is consistent with your core attributes, but also forces you to stretch a bit. Let us look at some familiar examples of dramatically different circumstances that can spur new learning and growth. For most people, heading off to freshman year in college creates a degree of destabilization. Students often discover in the first several weeks that what they thought were good study habits in high school, what they assumed were beliefs and values that most people held, and how they approached making friends, are perspectives not adhered to by everyone on their dorm floor.

Other major life events like marriage, death of a loved one, or the birth of children can also force people to accommodate internally in order to take into account dramatically different circumstances. As we discussed in the Introduction, the similarity across these types of events is that our internal cognitive framework often cannot incorporate the new circumstances; consequently, we must restructure our beliefs and thinking. Often, these types of situations can seem overwhelming, and the level of stress we feel can undermine our effectiveness.

The answer, however, is not to seek out situations where you never experience any level of stress or arousal. Situations where you are disinterested or detached might feel relaxing on some level, for some length of time, but ultimately you cannot generate enough energy to be highly effective in what you are doing. The key, as in the story of the three bears and Goldilocks, is to have a level of emotional arousal that is 'just right'.

The sweet spot. Most people would agree that there is a level of alertness that leads to their best performance, whether in sports, artistic endeavors, public speaking, or facilitating a team discussion. If you experience a low level of attentiveness or preparedness, you might come across as rather flat in your energy level. On the other hand, if you experience an enormous level of vigilance and tension before a particular situation, your performance will suffer. Somewhere in between is your 'sweet spot'.

Psychologists would call this sweet spot the optimal level of arousal. This is your apex of alertness, the place where you function with the utmost confidence and competence. Here, you are the most motivated and alert, and the fraud factor has very little effect on your successful achievement of desired outcomes. Because you function most effectively and comfortably in this sweet spot, you have a tendency to want to remain there and tap its full potential. Usually, that is a good thing and it feels like the right fit.

However, the right fit can evolve into the wrong fit over time. Sometimes you hunker down too long in this sweet spot of confidence and competence. You become complacent and stop stretching and growing. Because you experience your greatest feelings of success in your sweet spot, you tend to want to stay within these comfortable walls.

In your career, you may have experienced situations where you stayed too long in one job or with one company because it felt comfortable and seemed to fit the needs of your personal and family life. Often in these situations, you stop learning new skills and perspective and just coast for a while, because it feels so right. In fact, those who feel like a fraud often spend their maximum efforts in the areas where they have the greatest comfort and confidence, avoiding the other facets of their jobs.

A recent coaching client of mine, Anne, engaged in this behavior to such a degree in her job that it significantly inhibited her learning and growth. Over time, major problems had developed in one area of her responsibilities, and she had not handled them quickly nor effectively enough. Not surprisingly, the area she ignored was the one where she felt the least confident. *"I didn't know much about one of my new areas of responsibility,"* she confided, *"and the other three areas were having issues that I understood and could address confidently. So, I tended to spend my time on those. At first, my boss seemed to be happy with my work focus."*

Without realizing it, however, she had gravitated toward the most familiar functions, the ones where she felt least like a fraud. Her deflated sense of self and fears about failing in this new role had created a sort of blindness to problems in the other, less familiar, area of her work. Anne explained in our first meeting, *"The entire clinic was actually a turnaround situation, a fact that I was not fully aware of when I first interviewed for the job. One of the groups was particularly needy, and tended to act out in dysfunctional ways. I was spread way too thin in my role. For example, I had 60 performance reviews to write every six months, in addition to my other administrator functions! It was nearly impossible to stay on top of everything."*

As a consequence of having too many responsibilities pulling on her time, Anne focused on those areas where the fires were burning the hottest. A couple areas of her duties were not going very well, and she, in fact, turned them around. She also developed strong relationships with most of the physicians and many of the other healthcare professionals. It felt right to her.

Unfortunately, one of the smaller units of the clinic had one nurse in particular who engaged in problematic behaviors that had not been confronted by previous leadership. His behavior stirred up dysfunctional reactions in others on the staff, so Anne decided to confront him. She described what happened next by saying, *"Though I typically struggle with being assertive in situations like this, I found the courage to confront him and tell him that the behaviors I was observing had to stop, or his job was in jeopardy. Though he was a bit defensive, he seemed to handle the feedback and ultimatum well, and he appeared to be on board with the idea of changing his approach."*

After his meeting with Anne, however, he contacted an attorney and filed a harassment suit, citing a hostile work environment created by her actions. Before this suit could develop very far along, Anne's senior management decided that the quickest, least painful choice for them was to let her go. As we noted in an earlier chapter, frauds get fired.

She used the remainder of our coaching to help her understand that the underlying problem was her hesitance to assert herself when she felt uncertain. This position was a stretch for her, based on her previous experience, and that was a part of her deflated self-confidence. As a self-confessed, *"workaholic who tends to take on too much, get burned out, and not speak up about it,"* she had fallen into the same pattern in this new administrator role.

Because she had self-doubts about her ability to turn things around, Anne focused most of her attention early on in the areas where she was relatively confident. She was stretched well beyond what any one person could reasonably be expected to handle effectively, but she did not push back assertively about the situation. Her approach had left the problem nurse and department on its own for far too long. When she finally tried to step in, she did it in a more aggressive, rather than assertive, manner and created a hornet's nest of reaction.

This tendency to function where you are most comfortable can, as in Anne's case, lead to getting fired, or it can lead to a sense of atrophy and feelings of boredom. It can also lead to a dead-end in your career, or feelings of resignation in your life as you settle for something less exciting and fulfilling. New growth is critical to maintaining your competency edge; just like sharpening a knife is important, to keep it from becoming dull.

Anne's story illustrates that you can get comfortably stuck in your sweet spot. If you avoid situations that challenge you, it will likely minimize the degree to which you feel dissonance in your life. However, it will also minimize the degree to which you grow and become increasingly effective, and might even undermine your ability to take on new roles and responsibilities. Staying too long in your sweet spot can create a sense of ennui and lack of passion. As another of my coaching clients observed regarding his job, *"At first, I loved it and poured myself into it, but, later on, I got bored."* When you stay too long on the same road, variety, challenge, and new ideas are pushed to the curb.

What should you do to make sure you are functioning at your optimal level, stretching and growing, but still operating within your sweet spot of effectiveness? How can you make sure you do not caught up in fraudulent behaviors brought about by the Big Fat Lie? I suggest in the next chapters a three-step process in which you ask yourself the following questions:

- How do I get in my own way?
- Who am I at the core?
- How can I get real again?

QUESTIONS TO CONSIDER AND DISCUSS

➡ What do you believe your 'sweet spot' or sweet spots are in your work? How comfortable are you straying from that place?

➡ Have you ever missed some problem areas at work, or neglected some areas of your responsibilities, because you were too focused on your sweet spot? How did you work through that situation?

➡ How confident are you that your current role represents the 'right fit' for you? What contributes to your doubts about it being right?

HOW DO I GET
IN MY OWN WAY?

Core Concept: How do people get in their own way? What do they do that undermines their effectiveness, sometimes to the degree that others begin to question their abilities? These components are common across all who suffer from the destabilization created by feeling like a fraud:

- Encountering a stressful situation
- Reacting rather than responding
- Building structures that sustain the reaction
- Rationalizing the ROI on the reactive behaviors

As we discussed in a previous chapter, the most effective you will ever be happens when you lead competently and confidently as the person you are. In the next three chapters, we will dig more deeply into this idea, helping empower you to use new tools and strategies that will enable you to lead from your core. In this chapter, we look at how people like you can inadvertently get in their own way.

First, let's remind ourselves why leaders tend to stumble over this obstacle we are defining as 'the fraud factor'. They typically encounter situations that put them back on their heels and generate anxiety over whether or not they will truly be able to navigate them successfully. On some level, they feel like everything they know is wrong and insufficient to deal with the set of circumstances they face. Into that initial moment of anxious hesitation, a lie bubbles up from within. This lie, whatever its actual form may be, convinces them that they are incapable of working through a given situation. That's when they start to feel like a fraud and begin to exhibit behaviors that undermine their effectiveness.

So, how do leaders get in their own way? What do they do that undermines their effectiveness, sometimes to the degree that others begin to question their abilities in the role? Here are the components that I have observed in executives, common across all who suffer from the dissonance created by feeling like a fraud:

- Encountering a stressful situation
- Reacting rather than responding
- Building structures that sustain the reaction
- Rationalizing the ROI on the reactive behaviors

We will use Vern's story to illustrate how leaders get in their own way.

Encountering a stressful situation. When I started working with Vern, he had just been promoted to a Senior Director level at a manufacturer of custom glass products. He had worked in the industry for more than 15 years, and had been with his current employer for about three years. On his 360-degree feedback report, coworkers and manager described him as confident and self-assured, enthusiastic, humorous, and collaborative. They viewed him as a leader who fostered commitment in others, drove toward the desired results, and inspired top performance on his team. It was a very positive profile, with only a few suggestions for improvement, including listening better and being less direct at times.

One other set of ratings and comments stood out, however. A number of people indicated they felt that he needed to work on being less emotional in stressful situations. Vern and I discussed this feedback in greater depth, and he said that he thought this had become true in the past few years as he found himself in more and more unfamiliar situations that were farther and farther outside his sweet spot of experience. The circumstance that had become his lightning rod catalyst which spawned an emotional response, was speaking to groups of people at work.

Reacting rather than responding. Particularly when Vern found himself in situations where he was about to speak to a group of more than half a dozen people on a topic in which he felt he was not expert or prepared enough, he became overwhelmed with anxiety. His eyes would begin to dart back and forth, he would pull his thoughts way back inside his head, and he would begin to pace back and forth. Others around him would ask him what was wrong, because his behavior had changed in such a visibly dramatic way.

For him, this kind of situation generated anxiety and an irrational belief, as he stated it, "to *be the smartest person in the room to prove himself to be worthy of the VP title*." He feared that people would not respect him, otherwise. He was afraid that he would disappoint them, or not meet their expectations of him, thus they would think that he was stupid. If he was unable to talk himself down from this high level of anxiety, he would begin to look for ways to escape the room. If he was unable to avoid speaking, he would start talking at a very high rate of speed, throwing words into the space between him and the audience and hoping something smart would come out.

Building structures that sustain the reaction. As Vern grappled with this public speaking fear prior to us starting to work together in a coaching relationship, he created structures designed to minimize the negative impact. For example, he looked for excuses to explain why he should not speak, suggesting other people who could take his place. When he was unable to push the assignment to someone else, he would spend many hours in advance writing detailed notes and going over them so that he would feel fully prepared. He also talked with his manager and requested to be the first to speak, so that his anxiety would not get a chance to increase as his turn came around.

When in the actual speaking situation, he often started off the presentations with a question to the group or a joke about someone in the audience. Doing this seemed to him to help calm his nerves. In Vern's mind, these structures were designed to limit the damage he might cause to his image in others' eyes.

To a degree, they may have actually accomplished this. However, they also served to sustain his anxious reaction, because they did not deal with the underlying causes. He became someone who nervously and compulsively prepared for each speaking engagement, and, at the same time, continued to look for an escape hatch to avoid them.

Rationalizing the ROI on the reactive behaviors. To Vern, even though the behaviors in which he engaged did not address the underlying reason for his anxiety, they did seem to help him get through. Some speaking situations actually seemed to flow smoothly, without the intense anxiety and desire to flee. He would spend hours preparing and many anxious minutes worrying about how badly it might go, but he rationalized that these behaviors helped him. The return they appeared to provide at times seemed to him to justify the time and energy he put into them. Since, at the time, he did not have any better ideas for how to more effectively navigate his public speaking anxiety, he clung to them and continued to employ them. As we worked together in our coaching relationship, he began to recognize that the return on his investment of preparation and worry was disappointingly low. Over time, he was able to work through this fear consistently.

In a recent email I received from Vern, he said that all was good now on the business side of his life. He wrote, "*I have had numerous situations recently which in the past would have been hard for me to control, but now I'm much more assertive and I don't get all wacked out. I feel more confident, and I engage much more easily without the anxiety. Things are really going better!*"

Vern went on to write, "*I have signed up for a public speaking class with some of my co-workers through HR, which should help on that front, as well. It's funny that I see things so differently now. Some of those folks who I thought were so scary smart have way less to offer than I do. I'm not saying I still don't need improvement, but I'm not the dope I thought I was!*" Perspective is a funny thing, as it changes the way a person views him or herself within the context of the organization.

He ended the email with, "*I suspect that if we had started our coaching sessions prior to my promotion, some of the opportunities for change would have been different. All in all it has ended up being a wonderful experience to work through this. Basically it came down to what we both said— 'deal with it now or have it follow you around wherever you go'. Again, I still have a lot of room to improve, but at*

*least I feel I'm moving in the right direction. Thanks
for your help!"*

In a subsequent coaching session, we identified a
healthy leadership belief that he could use to help
him offset the irrational fear in these public speaking situations. We both laughed out loud when I
suggested as his new mantra, *"I suck less at this
than anyone else would."* This phrase continues to
provide him with a humorous counterbalance to his
public speaking fears.

LaToya provides another example of how these four
components affect leaders and create situations
where they get in their own way. The project manager for a mid-sized construction company, she had
worked in the field for many years. She had started
as a common laborer cleaning up the messes that
skilled workers left on the build site, and had doggedly pushed to take on more skilled work until the
guys around her began to recognize her abilities to
manage others, read blueprints, and solve problems.
Over time, she had become the 'go-to' superinten-
dent for the company's major building projects.

When I met her manager, he described her as accomplished, talented, and a quick study who understood complex engineering concepts, though she
was not formally trained. LaToya was one of his top

three project managers. However, she was viewed as a Type A, aggressive person, who used rough language, and did not suffer fools readily. The HR Director described her as 'foul-mouthed' and 'disrespectful' as well as lacking in polish, as a leader.

As I began to work with her, I recognized that certain circumstances she encountered were most likely to push her buttons. These included ones where the safety and well-being of workers was being compromised, where work quality was below standard, and where workers either lied to her or tried to mislead her. When these kinds of situations took place—and they often occurred multiple times in a single day—she would blow up. Often, she would threaten to fire or cause harm to certain parts of a worker's anatomy if they did not shape up. Instead of coming up with a reasonable, logical response to problems, she would react aggressively.

The structures that LaToya built to sustain the reactions were all internal rationalizations. She convinced herself that, if she did not come down hard on every infraction of safety, quality, deadlines, or timely follow-through, the workers and subcontractors on her building projects would not deliver what they promised. Consequently, she felt like she needed to whack them with a verbal hammer to achieve the results she had promised her bosses. This internal reasoning sustained her inappropriate reactions and approaches.

Every time she hammered someone verbally or threatened to fire them, they grudgingly did what she had directed them to do. To her, this just proved that she needed to be aggressive to make them follow through. The ROI in her mind was that her approach seemed to be working, and she did not have any other ideas about how to accomplish the same level of quality results. So, she continued to use the big hammer.

Then, something occurred that whacked her in the head and finally got her attention. She was put on a two-week suspension for threatening a worker, who then complained to the HR Director. Suddenly, the ROI seemed to drop significantly in her eyes, and she was open to talking to me. In our first coaching meeting, she was very skeptical. A previous attempt at a coaching relationship had not gone well. I told her, *"This is where smart—you—meets educated—me, and I think we will work very well together."* We then began to figure out a plan in which she could lead others in a way that met her needs, but did not leave bodies in her wake.

QUESTIONS TO CONSIDER AND DISCUSS

➥ What kinds of situations act as a catalyst for you, and push you into a reactive state of mind? What does it look like when you react to these types of situations; how does it feel on the inside?

➥ What tends to reinforce and sustain your ineffective reactions in your work? What do you tell yourself that keeps you using these approaches, even though you may not be achieving your desired results with others?

➥ What has been the ROI for you over the years in using a reactive approach to deal with circumstances you have faced? That is, what seems to have reinforced and prolonged your reactive behaviors?

WHO AM I
AT THE CORE?

Core Concept: Your core is the essence of who you are as a person, your true self, not the person you have become over time in order to be who you think others want you to be. As hard as you might try to change your stripes and become someone very different than the person you are, it will be a very frustrating and ultimately fruitless exercise. At your core is a combination of personality characteristics, feelings, intellectual and physical abilities, and a responsive spirit. There are also thoughts, beliefs, and opinions that you hold to be true, which you have developed since early childhood. Wherever you go, your core personality traits, abilities, spirit, and thinking go with you.

arlier in this book, I introduced the idea that to be as effective as you can be as a leader, you must lead from the core of who you really are. Your core is the essence of who you are as a person, your fundamental nucleus of unique characteristics that are consistent and enduring over time. This is your true self, not the person you have become over time in order to be who you think others want you to be. Some describe this self as *"the way God made you to be."*

Trying to be like someone else that you admire as a leader, who is very different from you, or trying to minimize your key attributes because you think they are not acceptable, are recipes for disaster. As hard as you might try to change your stripes and become someone very different than the person you are, it will be a very frustrating and ultimately fruitless exercise.

I first discovered this as a college freshman, walking down the street in Evanston, IL. As I walked to the library and considered my experience so far in college, it occurred to me that I did not need to be limited by my past from high school. Nobody from my graduating class had chosen Northwestern University; consequently, I had no baggage of previous impressions to limit me. Instead of being introverted and socially awkward, I could be outgoing and effervescent. Instead of being serious and studious, I could be fun-loving and unconcerned about grades. In short, I could choose to change my personality to become someone fundamentally different from the person I had been up to that point. I felt liberated!

The closer I got to the library, the more convinced I was of the beauty and possibility of this plan. I would change who I was at the core and become a BMOC (big man on campus), a bon vivant that no one would recognize when I returned home at Christmas break. I started to smile at the picture these thoughts painted inside my head. Thinking back to that moment, I am not so much smiling now, as I am laughing at myself for being so naïve! Okay, it is true that, during my four years in college, I became more outgoing and socially confident, put less emphasis on grades, and learned to laugh at situations (and, occasionally, at myself). However, I did not change the core of who I am. I changed some behaviors, perceptions, ideas, and strategies, but remained the same at my core.

The days and weeks after coming to my revelation in college showed me that, regardless of the circumstances around me and my desire for a fresh start, I remained the same at the center of my being. The characteristics, traits, and capacities that defined me did not change, for the most part. In that sense, I could not be anyone I wanted to be; I could not cut myself off from the past and create a new person from the ground up. Instead, I needed to embrace more fully the person I was at the core, and then I needed to more completely and confidently express me as that person.

To put it in simple terms, I needed to recognize that I was the product of my **PAST**:

- **P**ersonality
- **A**bility
- **S**pirit
- **T**hinking

As I have discovered since my musings on the way to the library, I function best in the present when I leverage my PAST. You also are a product of your PAST, and, as with me, it is the key to your future. At your core is a combination of personality characteristics, feelings, intellectual and physical abilities, and a responsive spirit. At the center of who you are, there are also thoughts, beliefs, and opinions that you hold to be true, which you have developed since early childhood.

Whether or not you are fully conscious of these factors at your core, they exist and they powerfully influence your behavior every day. Though it is possible in many ways to leave the past behind—through forgiving others, letting go of hurts, moving on in relationships, etc.—it is not feasible to leave your PAST behind. Wherever you go, your core personality traits, abilities, spirit, and thinking go with you.

Christine is a good example of how insight about her PAST was very helpful in her role as the Director of Operations for a manufacturing organization. On her 360-degree feedback results, the comments and ratings of others depicted her as a leader with high standards who was resourceful under stress and optimistic about achieving results, despite obstacles. Further, feedback givers saw her as confident and assertive, honest and straightforward, and realistic in her appraisals of situations.

Supporting these observations about her abilities and skills were Christine's personality test results, which described her as steady and consistent in the face of pressure, systematic and organized, deliberate and methodical as a decision-maker, and oriented toward achieving results at a high level of quality. Additional test results pictured her as outgoing and gregarious, practical and commonsense, and detail-oriented. Upon hearing this summary of her personality and style, Christine smiled and accepted the description as accurate. Then, she frowned a bit. When I asked her what the frown was about, she said that, while this picture was accurate and reassuring, her boss seemed to want her to be someone very different in her role.

Christine explained that, because of conflicting expectations and feedback on her style between her boss and his boss, she was becoming confused about how they wanted her to carry out her role. One of them wanted her to be direct and results-oriented, and he appreciated her dispassionate and logical orientation when crises occurred. The other one was critical of her lack of empathy for people and wanted her to be more appreciative of others' efforts and more aware of the impact of her words—even when they were not successfully carrying out their duties or following through on what they promised to deliver. Consequently, Christine had been going through a bit of occupational schizophrenia as she tried to shift her personality and approach. This made her appear 'disingenuous' as one feedback giver phrased it.

As we began to work in our coaching engagement, focusing on who she was at the core gave Christine a solid stepping-off place to begin to change some of the specific techniques and approaches she was using with people. She recognized that, given her signature personality traits, she would probably never come across as warm and fuzzy to her team or peers. However, she could leverage her style in ways that: built trust through consistent alignment of her words and behavior, encouraged others to follow her confident goal-oriented approach, and raised the team's self-assurance to consistently achieve high quality results.

Together, Christine and I looked at each of the four core facets of personality, abilities, spirit, and thinking, and used the insight to help her lead confidently. Let me describe each of these in greater detail, so that you can better understand and apply them to yourself.

Personality. Representing the first letter of the word PAST, 'P' is 'personality'—a word that most people recognize. However, few agree on a definition. When people say, "*She has a great personality,*" or "*His personality just doesn't click with mine,*" we have a vague concept of what they mean. We usually need to ask for clarification to make sure we have an unambiguous understanding of the meaning. That is due to the broad and sometimes confusing nature of the term 'personality'.

From the field of psychology, we know that some theorists and clinicians think of personality in terms of 'the primary psychological processes' present in a person. Some talk in terms of the dynamic interplay of these processes, others in terms of individual differences evident across people, and still others look at it in terms of similarities in human nature that are evident in groups of people.

The word personality comes originally from the Latin word 'persona', which refers to an individual's identity. Personality is a dynamic and organized set of traits or characteristics that influence the way people think, feel, and behave. There is little theoretical agreement among psychologists, let alone the general population, on what personality actually is.

For the purposes of your own self-analysis, consider the aspects of your personality that uniquely define you. This includes characteristics like:
- approach across various situations
- intensity of observable energy, degree of drive, level of motivation
- self-discipline, accountability, preference for structure
- 'signature' qualities that are consistent and distinct
- emotions, feelings, degree of compassion
- interpersonal orientation (introverted versus extroverted, for example)

Though extremely helpful, it is not necessary to engage in a formal personality assessment to identify and embrace your fundamental attributes. You can simply ask yourself, *"What are my signature traits and characteristics, the ones most central to my style?"* If you have not given this much thought, this might be a challenging question. One way to get to an answer is to think about the ways in which you see yourself as different or distinct from your friends, work peers, or relatives. What stands out about you relative to others? What characteristics are the most consistent in your style?

If your mind is blank on this, send an email to 10 of your closest friends, coworkers, and relatives, asking them to write down the first five to 10 words or phrases that come to mind when they think of you. The words you receive in response typically will be personality characteristics such as: being friendly, caring about people, confident in your perspective, decisive, having high integrity, or highly motivated. Then, synthesize these words into the top five to 10 most consistent words and phrases across the group of responses. The result is a list of 'signature characteristics' that others who know you well recognize as unique to you.

Why is it important to identify your signature personality qualities? One key reason is that it will help you understand how you are likely to come across to others as you lead or interact with them. Another is that, since you cannot change your fundamental personality, the best you can do is to understand yourself at a deep level, embrace who you are, and leverage your core personality traits as much as possible.

Abilities. In many ways, the word 'ability' is as difficult to define as personality. Some psychologists, including me, use 'abilities tests' to measure an individual's capacity in areas such as verbal, numerical, and spatial reasoning. Others talk about multiple intelligences that include verbal, logical, interpersonal, kinesthetic, musical, visual, and more. Still others have developed tests and a theoretical framework that emphasize the importance of emotional intelligence, or EQ, over that of cognitive intelligence, or IQ. Psychologists also speculate about innate capacities that are sometimes called 'aptitudes', and other times 'talents'. A few psychologists and therapists, and a number of clergy and religious leaders, talk about gifts, both natural and spiritual.

For our purposes, all of these fit under the general umbrella term of 'abilities', which is the 'A' letter of the word PAST. Included in this are your innate talents, gifts, natural physical capacity, motivated strengths, cognitive intelligence, and emotional intelligence. The primary distinction we will make here is that abilities are innate capacities, not learned ones. Certainly, people develop their abilities over time, and those that receive the most attention tend to be their strongest, most recognizable abilities. However, we will draw a clear line to distinguish between the knowledge and skills you develop, versus abilities, talents, or gifts you have possessed from an early age. Skills and knowledge can shift dramatically over your lifetime, but your fundamental abilities do not change much.

Thinking about yourself as a leader, there is also a clear distinction between the competencies you may exhibit in leading others and your underlying ability to lead. What are some examples of fundamental leadership abilities? Words like communicator, wise counselor, visionary, interpersonal facilitator, educator/guide, motivator, or initiator reflect underlying capacities that can be expressed and observed in your outward behaviors and actions. Using this partial list of fundamental abilities as a starting point, what are your most motivated abilities as a leader? What do you do easily, that comes naturally to you and energizes you? What abilities do others, such as peers, direct reports, and manager most appreciate about you; what strengths do they leverage most often when involving you on team projects?

We have learned from the Gallup Organization over the years, and from others, that leaders are most effective when functioning within their strengths, or motivated abilities. That is, when you as a leader leverage your natural talents, you function at peak effectiveness and experience optimal satisfaction in your work. Combining effectiveness and satisfaction is a powerful recipe for success.

Spirit. The word 'spirit' perfectly captures the essence of what I want to convey here, yet it is an awkward and easily misunderstood term. It represents the 'S' in your PAST. Most people can describe the feeling they get when their spirit is uplifted by an event or circumstance around them, just as they can describe the feeling they have when their spirit is downcast or pessimistic. Spirit is something you can feel when it is moved by events or circumstances around you, but it is difficult to put into words. Perhaps that is because the English word 'spirit' comes from the Latin word 'spiritus', which means 'breath', but also can mean 'soul', 'courage', or 'vigor'. The variety of possible meanings can be confusing as we attempt to create a common understanding for the purposes of this book.

Here, we will use the word spirit to refer to an entity that has no physical substance, but, rather, an ethereal quality. It cannot be measured, but the effects of it can be perceived by the person whose spirit is aroused, as well as by outside observers in many instances. Your spirit develops from a very early age—perhaps at birth or even in the womb—and grows to become an integral aspect of your core being. In popular theological terms, the individual human spirit is a deeply situated, core aspect of the individual, subject to spiritual growth. In many ways, it is the very center of your capacity for joy and passion.

Unlike animals, humans have a spiritual nature that responds to something larger than and outside of themselves. For example, when gazing upon the Grand Canyon, most of us experience a spiritual sense of awe at the magnitude and beauty of what we observe as Nature or God's Creation. Similarly, when walking along an ocean or a path in the foothills of a mountain, our spirits respond to the power and enormity of the vista. Often, when playing instruments, singing, or listening to music, our spirits respond powerfully to the combinations of notes and lyrics.

When praying or meditating, or in any way resonating to the miraculous, our spirits leap inside us. Christians talk about spirit in terms of the 'fruits of the spirit' that include love, joy, peace, patience, kindness, goodness, faithfulness, gentleness, and self-control. Judeo-Christian believers emphasize a deep relationship with God, with some emphasizing an intense, personal relationship as a way of experiencing this spirit. For our purposes in this book, the spiritual aspect of your core includes your sense of purpose and life meaning, your source of joy and peace, and your wellspring of passion and enthusiasm.

Spiritual refreshment is one way you can think about the spirit component of your core. Consider what gives you the greatest sense of calm, relaxation, or inner peace, or which activities in your life reso-nate within you in a way that leaves you composed, unruffled, or serene. Think about the times when you experience the greatest feeling of tranquility and har-mony with the world around you. These are moments when your spirit is nourished.

Alternatively, you can think about the times when you are most energized and excited in your work and life. Note the tasks or activities that bring out the most intense feelings of joy, elation, and well-being, and the people that delight you and bring you the greatest enjoyment or amusement. Consider when you feel the most happy in your work, or in your life in general.

A third avenue to discover the spiritual core of your-self is to determine when you have the most sense that your life has meaning. Think about what you do that brings out the recognition inside you that your life matters; reflect on which activities in your work and family time seem most central to your life pur-pose. Whether you think about purpose from the perspective of a calling from God on your life (the original meaning of the word 'vocation'), or a calling determined within your own heart and mind, purpose is central to the spirit part of your core. Functioning within your purpose, and living a life that feels like it matters and has meaning, feeds your spirit. However, when you operate far from your sense of purpose and meaning, it creates a sense of agitation, emptiness, and weariness in your spirit.

The three core components we have looked at so far, personality, abilities, and spirit, tend to be relatively stable in adults. They do not change much, if at all, after early adulthood, though you may continue to discover previously unexplored or unknown aspects of each of them as you get to know yourself during your middle and later adult years. This is merely the natural process of self-development and discovery as you age, not the appearance of entirely new personality traits or fundamental abilities.

Thinking. On the other hand, the thinking aspect of your core tends to change throughout life as you encounter new information and perspective that no longer can be explained or understood by your previous ways of thought. Of the four core components of a leader, thinking is the one you can consciously develop to the greatest degree. Thinking is the last letter of your PAST, and the aspect of your core that is typically most apparent to people around you.

Precisely what do we mean by the word 'thinking'? This component includes your beliefs, values, and opinions based on your learning and experience. It includes your attitudes toward things, the way you make sense of the world, and the primary basis upon which you make decisions. Thinking includes logic and intuition, creativity and originality, common sense, and the recognition and understanding of others' feelings and needs. In short, thinking includes any function within your core that involves thought processes.

Some of your thoughts provide the foundation for your most effective leadership, and some become obstacles. From the point of view of cognitive-behavioral psychology, every action you take in your work and non-work life receives direction from your thought processes. You get upset with someone, for example, based on whether or not you think their behavior or words are directed at you, and your specific response is directed by your beliefs and attitudes. The bottom line is that your beliefs give direction and energy to your behavior.

As a leader, then, you must become aware as fully as possible of the thoughts, attitudes, beliefs, and values inside your head that direct your behavior. Leaders who successfully lead from their core exhibit behaviors driven by reasonable, rational beliefs. We will call this 'effective thinking'. As much as possible, your goal should be to lead based on your most effective thinking, the kind that directs your high performance behaviors.

What does high performance look like? Many people I have coached describe their high performance behaviors like this:
- decisive, action-oriented
- confident and optimistic
- focused and clear-thinking
- collaborative, deeply listening
- compassionate and thoughtful

To better understand effective leadership thinking, it is helpful to differentiate between thoughts about yourself as a leader and thoughts about the people you lead. Both must be effective in order to be successful at leading from the core.

Here are some examples of effective thinking about self:

- I can usually figure out an answer to the problems I face.
- I am capable of building competence in my team members.
- I am trustworthy, because I genuinely care about others.
- I will never be too old to learn something new.
- It's never too late to do the right thing.
- I can let go of the control of things, turn it over to God.
- I am assertive and confident at my core.

And, here are some examples of effective thinking about others:

- Everyone has personal struggles and these can affect performance.
- It is possible to bring out the best in people by appealing to their hearts.
- People generally want to do the right thing, but do not always know what that is.
- If I surround myself with the brightest and hardest working people, we will bring out the best in each other.
- Others will reach their potential if given enough time, patience, and compassion by their leader.
- People mean well, but they sometimes need guidance to do the right thing.

In my coaching work with leaders at multiple levels across a wide variety of organizations, I have found that this area of thinking offers the most possibility for new growth. It is here that you can develop healthier beliefs and identify those self-limiting beliefs that undermine your effectiveness. Thinking is also the lever you can work to improve the problem solving of others. Helping people on your team think differently, consider other options, and question their own self-limiting talk can nurture their growth into more effective leaders.

As we discussed in earlier chapters, the Big Fat Lie is an example of self-limiting talk that undermines high performance behaviors. Further, when you interact with others out of your faulty, ineffective beliefs, you tend to create negative reactions in these others, which gets in the way of successful work relationships. For a more complete discussion of this phenomenon, see my book, **Fearless Leadership** (Leader Press, 2006).

With this deeper understanding of how your PAST informs who you are at the core, the next step is to leverage this perspective and use it to become a more genuine and authentic leader. It's time to get real again. You can do this!

QUESTIONS TO CONSIDER AND DISCUSS

➥ What do you see as your unique personality traits?

➥ When you consider your signature abilities, which ones stand out?

➥ For the core component of spirit, think about what most energizes you or gives you the greatest sense of satisfaction or excitement in your life. How does work tap into your sense of life purpose and meaning, your inspirations, and your feelings of joy, peace, or acceptance? Which of these spiritual aspects of you permeate your leadership approach?

➥ What are some examples of your most effective thinking about yourself as a leader, and about leading others?

HOW CAN I GET REAL AGAIN?

Core Concept: The process of getting real again as a person involves recognizing and leveraging your unique personality traits and abilities, finding ways to feed your spirit, and analyzing your thought patterns to discern and apply those that are most highly effective. Change your thinking, and you will augment an important aspect of the core of who you are as a person and as a leader. Of the four key elements of your core (Personality, Abilities, Spirit, and Thinking), thinking is the only one that is amenable to genuine transformation as an adult.

T he process of getting real again involves recognizing and leveraging your unique personality traits and abilities, finding ways to feed your spirit, and analyzing your thought patterns to discern and apply those that are most highly effective. This section of the book will help you develop a strategy for doing just that.

Recognizing, leveraging personality. We met Christine in the previous chapter of this book. Much of my work with her centered on the distinction between her core personality characteristics and what specific strategies and techniques she should employ to be effective at the highest level. In interpreting her feedback from others, I believed that the core attributes she brought to the table were important to her team and the larger organization; I wanted to make very certain that she felt affirmed in them. However, I also knew that she needed to utilize different strategies in some cases and specific techniques in other cases to influence and align people.

In her organization, Christine possessed a rare combination of strategic perspective, sense of urgency, capacity to prioritize and recognize critical customer issues, and drive for results. I did not want to do anything to diminish those capabilities, so, we started by drawing the picture of who she was at the core. Once she understood this picture fully, we shifted our focus to learning and employing new approaches to express her point of view, enroll others, and develop her team.

Like Christine, it is important for you to distinguish between your core personality characteristics, which do not change, and the particular strategies and behaviors you employ as you interact with others. My experience tells me that people tend to fall into three buckets when it comes to knowing their signature personality characteristics. Some are relatively disinterested, having not given it much thought and not developed much insight about it. A second group has a strong set of beliefs about their personalities, but the picture they paint inside their own heads does not match how other people see them. They are relatively oblivious. The third, and fortunately the largest group of people with whom I have worked, has a clear and accurate sense of their core personality traits. Hopefully, you are in this third bucket!

Often, leaders must develop strategies not natural to their core personalities, in order to be highly effective. Most introverted leaders, for example, learn to value their inner world perspective, but also develop a social style and skill set that enables them to better interface with others. Extroverted leaders, on the other hand, recognize the importance of using their outgoing style in meeting new people and helping others become comfortable in a social setting, but they also work to develop the capacity to leave space in conversations. For example, they learn to wait 10 seconds after they ask a question, before jumping in to answer it themselves. They remain the same at the core, but shift their approach somewhat to better fit the environment around them that typically includes both introverts and extroverts.

When I first started working with Sanjay, for example, he had received some direct feedback on a 360-degree instrument. His raters suggested that he needed to *"dial down the emotion and over-reaction,"* and to *"think about the impact of his words before jumping in to speak."* Others suggested that he work to *"bring down the temperature in stressful situations,"* and that he remain *"as cool and calm as possible."* These comments surprised and offended Sanjay, because he saw himself in an entirely different way. Adding to his confusion were comments about things his raters most appreciated about him, which included:

- Creative input and out of the box, visionary perspective
- Passion, energy, enthusiasm
- Willingness to take risks
- Smart, intuitive strategic thinking

From their comments and ratings, it seemed that Sanjay came across as a bit of a Jekyll and Hyde.

When we looked at his personality inventories, his scores showed a great deal of confidence and capacity to interact effectively with people. He clearly trusted people, was open and tolerant of their differing ideas, put a high degree of importance on building and maintaining quality relationships, and empathized with their needs and motivations.

When he leveraged these personality characteristics, his direct reports, peers, and others loved his style and wanted to draw closer to him as a leader. However, when he was in 'reaction mode', they viewed him as a poor listener who crossed boundaries, weighed in too quickly with his perspective, showed little empathy, came across as arrogant and dismissive, and was overly emotional. We decided to dig a bit deeper to discover the root of his over-reactions.

Sanjay was the oldest of three children whose parents had a tempestuous relationship, fueled in part by their father's alcoholism and violent temper. Sanjay remembered times when his parents were both drunk and got into fights with other adults who were present. When he was 7 years old, his mother left his father and took the children with her. Sanjay remembered that there was very little money for the family of four, and his grandparents helped out financially. While Sanjay was still living at home, his mother became involved in a lesbian relationship. The other woman was often violent and abusive to him and his younger siblings. He reported feeling that he barely survived his childhood.

These early family experiences undermined Sanjay's core personality and created an anxiety around people who seemed to be trying to take advantage of him or to diminish his value in some way. Every time someone at work raised a question about his tasks and responsibilities, he interpreted it as attacking him personally and became defensive. He was afraid that people would not like him once they got to know him, so he protected himself with a prickly exterior to make sure he would not get hurt again. In addition, he confessed that he falsely believed, "*I must please people all the time, or they won't love me.*" The resulting confusion from this underlying set of needs, fears, and beliefs left little room for his true personality to come out when he was in reactive mode.

Sanjay and I worked on two levels in our coaching relationship. On one level, we focused on his core personality traits and characteristics and how to recognize and nurture these in interactions with others. We emphasized the facets in his 360-degree feedback that his coworkers most appreciated about him, because these were the aspects that were most central to his genuine style. At the same time, we looked more deeply at his faulty beliefs about himself, like needing to please others all the time, and we began to replace these with healthy beliefs.

This was the first step to getting real again for Sanjay. Similarly, recognizing and identifying your core personality traits will help ground you to the foundation from which you should lead every day. Knowing your unique fingerprint of traits and characteristics and embracing them as your core will give you a bedrock platform to stand upon.

Recognizing, leveraging abilities. One of the questions leaders typically ask me is how they can leverage their strengths. That is, how can they take what they are really good at—particularly where they have underlying abilities—and become even better? For example, if they easily see the end result from the beginning, and they can identify every step that must occur on the pathway to get there, how can they use this strength more consistently and effectively? If they have a deep level of compassion and understanding for others and a knack for finding ways to help their team members develop, how can they leverage that ability? Or, if they are able to quickly see the potential flaws in a product, how can they apply that capacity more broadly and effectively in their work?

In my coaching, I often focus on leveraging underlying abilities and growing strengths. I have come to recognize that there are three basic ways to optimize these areas:

- dialing in
- dialing up
- dialing back

For some leaders, the identified need is **dialing in** to their underlying abilities, that is, to become more aware of them and comfortable with them. For example, I have worked with a number of people who were told that they must think more strategically, but they have had little understanding of what others mean by this and no sense of how to proceed. In these situations, we usually start by identifying what 'strategic' means in their organization, and which leaders seem to be most strategic from the organization's point of view.

Once we have a clear sense of the understood meaning of the word strategic, we focus on the ways in which they are already strategic in their thoughts and actions. Then, we develop new approaches, often involving the kinds of questions they pose and the amount of time they spend with good strategic thinkers. These methods typically help them hone their strategic thinking.

Wanda, for example, complained to me that she was "just not strategic" in her thinking. The observations of people around her, particularly her boss, seemed to confirm this self-concept. She had been criticized in a recent performance discussion for not putting enough focus on strategy or presenting a compelling enough big picture point of view. As a result, she felt demoralized and overwhelmed with how to increase her ability in that area. We started by talking about how much time she spent on big picture issues, and it became clear that she had inherited a rather inexperienced team. Consequently, she had spent most of the last two years trying to build their skills. At the same time, she had expended a large amount of time handling low-level details that she did not trust her team members to complete.

As Wanda and I talked, we recognized that her circumstances in the last couple of years had pushed her into a non-strategic corner, and there were several steps she would need to take to dial in to her strategic capacities. First, she needed to delegate more to her team members and literally put time on her calendar to work on big picture issues. Second, she needed to tap into the strategic thinking of her peers and others across the organization, and to notice how they approached situations and what they found most important. Third, she would need to become proficient at asking a set of questions that would help her uncover the strategic, big picture issues in most situations. We worked on all three of these areas together. Once she had more time to focus on the big picture, tapped into others who thought strategically, and learned to ask questions that brought out the strategic issues, she began to shift the perceptions of others.

For a second set of leaders, I help them leverage their abilities by **dialing up** the intensity and frequency in which they use certain competencies. In these cases, leaders are usually aware of their strengths in particular areas, but they are under-utilizing them from their organization's perspective. Often, they have some ineffective beliefs about using a particular strength, and some irrational fear about what will happen if they use certain approaches in the workplace. Once we work to get past these internal stumbling blocks regarding the proper use of their abilities, they usually are able to dial up the degree to which they employ them.

Calvin is a powerful example of this dialing up process. A tall and large-boned man, he had played college basketball under the hoop and was a somewhat physically intimidating figure. When he was growing up, he was the largest kid in most of his grades, and much larger than his two sisters. Consequently, his mother had emphasized repeatedly the directive that he was never to use his size to intimidate others or push to get his way.

This worked well at home and on the elementary school playground, but as an adult, Calvin had become meek in his interactions with others on the senior team. He had taken on the role of smooth mediator with his peers and his direct reports, which sometimes worked effectively, but, too often, made him come across as too indirect and hesitant to take a stand.

On his 360-degree feedback report, Calvin was depicted by others as someone who was often ineffective at asserting his point of view. They believed, based on his behaviors, that he lacked a sense of urgency and drive to accomplish tasks. They suggested in their comments that he *"become more of a leader," "challenge the business to improve,"* and *"give more direction to those who require it."* His passive, mediator approach to conflict also got in the way of the clarity of his communication. His boss suggested he, *"improve communication skills and build trust,"* while his peers called for him to deliver messages that were *"clear and straight out."*

The irony with Calvin is that his personality profiles depicted him as naturally very outgoing, energetic, confident, action-oriented, and focused on results. Clearly, he had the personality and abilities to be a strong leader who could challenge the status quo, achieve results, and communicate directly. However, because of his ineffective faulty beliefs about not intimidating others or pushing to get his way, he had dialed way back in the directness of his style. This was a problem for him at work, as evidenced by his 360-degree feedback results, but was also a problem at home. He reported that his wife was very agitated with him because she felt he did not take a firm enough stand with their two teenage daughters and college-aged son.

My strategy with Calvin was to help him recognize and unleash his fundamental abilities as reflected in the strengths part of his 360-degree feedback. Raters viewed him as smart and knowledgeable, ethical and values-driven, confident, honest, direct, open, innovative, and humorous. In reading this picture of him, he recognized that the raters had captured the essence of his self-perception of his strengths. I asked him what got in the way of him exhibiting this person at work and home on a consistent basis, and his response came back to his beliefs about holding himself in check so that he would not hurt others. From my perspective, it was time to unleash his strengths and use them powerfully. It was time for dialing up the utilization of his core abilities.

With a third set of leaders, our work involves **dialing back** their expression of strengths in their work. Usually, this occurs as a result of a leader coming on too powerfully and aggressively for the culture of the organization. These are often leaders who have keen strategic vision, a strong sense of urgency, and a focused drive to achieve results. They are typically resourceful, persistent, and unwavering, which can irritate and annoy others who approach problems and solutions from a much more deliberate, methodical, and cautious perspective. Sometimes, however, the strengths we need to dial back are soft abilities like compassion, empathy, and collaboration. In these cases, leaders focus on keeping relationships whole, empowering others, and working toward consensus, but lose sight of the urgency of achieving results and moving forward even when they cannot achieve full agreement.

As an example, Tom's personality and abilities testing depicted him as a strong, driven type who had the capacity to be tenacious, confident, and assertive. Inclined to take action and focused on results, he was strategic and dependable in his work, and confident in his recommendations for change. Often charismatic in his personal style, he could rally people around a concept and logically persuade them to his point of view. However, he often came across as frustrated and impatient with the lack of urgency in others' decisions and actions, and unwilling to let colleagues win arguments or discussions. Described by his boss as "*a bull in a china shop*," he had been overlooked several times for promotions because his dominating style caused him to lack credibility with senior leadership.

Tom had burned a number of bridges by the time we began working together, and he was smart enough to know that he needed to make major changes in his approach if he ever hoped to receive a promotion. We started with the delicate work of separating his underlying abilities from the ineffective strategies and techniques he had been using to prove a point and get his way. Starting with the faulty beliefs that drove his behavior, we began to paint a picture of the elements that eroded his effectiveness.

We also clearly outlined the unusual strengths he had, which he needed to continue to leverage in a dialed-back mode. He caught on quickly and was able to verbalize what he planned to do to dial back the intensity. As with all behavior change, however, it was a painstaking and time-consuming process to shift his actions and reactions, day to day, in a way that others came to recognize as a positive change. After about four months, his manager began to see the changes and trusted that Tom would not go back to his former aggressive approach.

Whether your core abilities need to be dialed in, dialed up, or dialed back, as you lead others, it is essential to make sure that you thoroughly tap into your signature strengths.

As we have emphasized throughout this book, to try to function outside your most motivated abilities is a frustrating and ultimately fruitless endeavor. It is important, then, to identify your underlying abilities and to leverage them powerfully in your work.

Understanding your spirit. Looking more deeply at the spirit part of your core can be a difficult and elusive exercise. For example, in my work with Jolene, we had to dig through a number of superficial layers before we got down to the nucleus of what feeds her spiritual side. Jolene worked as a consultant for a large IT consulting firm, with clients across the U.S. She had the reputation for being disorganized in her work and seemingly unconcerned about deadlines or scheduled meetings—at least internally. With her external clients, she was engaging and brilliant, often sacrificing her personal life to meet even the most outrageous demands to respond in a timely manner. She traveled extensively for her job, and was seldom in her office or home.

Jolene's prolonged periods of absence from the office and home only partially explained the disheveled appearance of each. Her office had piles upon piles of papers, client memos, and manuscripts related to IT. In fact, she was writing a book on IT consulting, and one of those documents, within one of the piles, was her unfinished text. Other consultants and her boss frequently made comments to her and to each other about the disorganized appearance of her office—assuming that the chaos must also reflect her state of mind.

I observed the condition of her office and was shocked that anyone could do any work there at all. It reminded me of the office of my doctoral advisor, who had to clear off a spot for me to sit each time we met. On the top of one of his piles was a small framed poster that read, *"Those who keep a neat and orderly work space never know the thrill of finding something they thought was irretrievably lost!"* I felt irretrievable lost in Jolene's office the only time we met there.

Through further conversation, however, I soon found out that her office was organized and tidy compared to her house. Jolene lived in a two-story home in the suburbs of a major metropolitan area with a large Persian cat named Mimi. She confessed that she put a bell around the cat's neck so that she could find her in her home. The two floors of the residence were covered, except for narrow walk spaces, with piles of boxes, unopened and undelivered gifts, books, and suitcases. Her closets were filled to the point of being unusable, in some cases with clothes that still bore the price tags and had never been worn.

It was difficult for me to imagine any sense of peace and well-being in such an environment, and Jolene was grappling with this, as well. She was also struggling with attention-deficit disorder (ADD) and a relatively rare form of obsessive-compulsive disorder, commonly called 'hoarding'. Though I do not work as a clinical psychologist, I found out that with ADD and hoarding, part of the treatment regimen is to chip away at the mess and provide consistent structure. She admitted that her home environment, in particular, was overwhelming, discouraging, and demotivating to her spirit. The problem I faced was how to tap into her spirit in a way that would help motivate her out of the chaos in which she lived and worked.

First, we generated a prioritized list of things she needed to do. The list contained entries like filing several years of back, unpaid taxes, ordering storage bins for her outside tools and implements, giving away boxes of stuff to a charity of her choice, and organizing her closets. To do this, we identified resources and friends who could help. She began to chip away at the mess one step at a time, with regular slips backward.

Once we had a new system in place, we began to discuss the aspects of her work and life that most fed her spirit. Work was easy—the interactions she had with clients and leveraging her expertise in the IT field were key satisfiers. Next, we discussed a list of 'refreshers' in her non-work life, most of which she had not done for months or years. A partial list of Jolene's spirit refreshers included:

- Reading mysteries or other novels
- Pampering herself with manicures or pedicures
- Going out to dinner or concerts with friends
- Watching baseball games at the stadium
- Traveling to new, offbeat places on vacation
- Engaging in painting or photography
- Taking energetic walks in the morning
- Worshiping at her church

Then, we developed a plan to re-introduce these refreshing activities on the weekends. This meant that she would need to stop dawdling with work-related projects on Saturdays and Sundays. Instead, she would plan fun activities that would refresh her spiritually. As Jolene took these baby steps toward spiritual replenishment by going out with friends, attending church, and taking walks again in the morning, she also found that she had renewed energy to work with her clients and finish her manuscript so it could be published. Once she re-discovered and began to nourish who she was at the core spiritually,

Jolene was able to leverage this realization in the other aspects of her work and life.

Understanding how your spirit permeates your approach to leadership is another key piece to the puzzle of who you genuinely are. It is critical in order for you to function at your highest level of energy and effectiveness. For example, if your spiritual focus comes from the Christian faith, people around you should be able to sense that your faith informs your approach to leadership. Spirit is critical because it includes your sense of purpose and life meaning, your source of joy and peace, and your wellspring of passion and enthusiasm. It should be the heart of your leadership approach, so that people around you can respond to it on a heart level.

Thinking more effectively. In this final aspect of leveraging your PAST, we look at how you can change the way you think about things, the beliefs you hold about others and yourself, and the attitudes you have adopted over time. Unlike your personality, abilities, and spirit, thinking is the one variable that you can work to consciously change over time. Spirit also can be consciously formed and developed to a degree—for example, as you turn your worry over to God. However, changes in your thinking are often the changes that can be leveraged the most in improving your effectiveness.

When I first started working with Mary, for example, she believed that she needed to prove to people that she always knew what she was talking about. Her thoughts about others were mostly focused on how they might turn on her if she messed up. She felt that she needed to overcompensate for being a female in a male-dominated engineering company by preparing fully, putting in extra time, and justifying her position. From her perspective, she needed to develop an 'edge' with others to make sure they respected her when she weighed in on a topic.

Based on her 360-degree feedback, this strategy was not working for her very well, so we talked about who she was in terms of her personality, abilities, and spirit. This helped her become grounded and reconnected to her core as a leader. Then, we began to address the thinking that undergirded her managerial role. She recognized quickly that the thinking that had motivated her actions in recent projects was not her 'best stuff', and that she had lost political capital in the way she had carried out her role.

This led Mary to create a new set of beliefs that reflected her behavior when she was the most effective and successful in her work. Here are two beliefs she developed to guide her in the future as a leader:

- If I give people clear indications that I'm listening and valuing their input (and don't think about myself or how well I am doing), they will truly value the interaction.

- When I let others step in to drive the process, and I provide needed resources for them, the whole team will be successful.

A very different set of circumstances was involved in Devon's work as a leader. He managed the customer service department of a med-tech manufacturer, where complaints and issues from sales people and healthcare professionals were daily occurrences. Before we began working together in a coaching relationship, his management of the team was based on him thinking he must be totally responsible, ask the right questions, and hold himself and others to high standards to make sure nothing bad happened. It was difficult for him to delegate work fully to his team members. Further, when he was not sure he would add value or present an interesting enough perspective in a discussion with peers or superiors, he believed he needed to clam up so he did not say something stupid.

When Devon and I began to talk about effective beliefs that could counter-balance these other beliefs which he had developed over time, at first he was rather perplexed. Once we started discussing his approach in high performance situations he encountered, however, he recognized a very different set of beliefs guiding his behavior. They included these:

- When I let go of things and delegate them to my direct reports, they can grow to the next level and I can work on higher level problems.

- My opinion matters and what I have to say will help the organization become even more successful.

- When I express my opinion, even if it is an opposing point of view, I can present it directly and assertively, in a way that others are open to hearing it and will respect me for saying it.

At that point in our work together, Devon's job was to become increasingly better at using these effective beliefs to guide his management style. As he began to do that consistently, he recognized how much more capable he was as a leader to his team and an influencer to senior management.

In the previous section of this chapter, I introduced Sanjay, discussing how his faulty beliefs and reactive behaviors made it difficult for others to value his genuine personality and style. In working together, we identified two effective beliefs that could guide his leadership style going forward. The two beliefs were:

- Trust is built on open communication and consistent behavior.
- I can influence people in my life by encouraging the behavior I want to see more of in them.

As he began to replace faulty beliefs and irrational reactions with a genuine interest in others and these two healthy beliefs, Sanjay's leadership approach changed dramatically for the better. At the conclusion of the coaching relationship, in a final meeting with his manager, Becky, she indicated that she no longer saw the strong, whipped-up, and angry reactions on Sanjay's part. She appreciated that he now expressed his concerns in a clear, rational way, and that he tended to "*hold his fire*" and consider situations thoroughly, before he came out with a thoughtful, logical response.

The beliefs that guide your leadership of others are probably a combination of thinking about your natural, most effective approaches to leadership, and thinking about others and how they best respond to being led. We offered examples of this kind of thinking in the previous chapter.

One way to develop your own effective beliefs is to consider how you ideally would like to respond in stressful situations, and then create a statement to reflect that. A simple approach to structure such a belief in your mind is to begin the sentence with, *"When I"* and follow that with a specific attitude, belief, or behavior that you know is part of your high performance responses. Then, end the sentence with what your experience or intuition tells you the hopeful, optimistic result will be. For example, you could say, *"When I listen to others and look for common ground, I will more likely lead them to a collaborative solution."*

As you carry out your leadership responsibilities, effective, healthy beliefs need to be at the very core of your thinking. Any other thinking will make you less effective and possibly lead to behaviors that undermine or derail your effectiveness. Change your thinking, and you will augment an important aspect of the core of who you are as a leader. Thinking is the only element of your core that is amenable to genuine transformation. Developing new, healthier beliefs is the way to transform your thinking.

QUESTIONS TO CONSIDER AND DISCUSS

➡ What do you perceive stands in the way of you being as real, genuine, and authentic as you could be in your leadership role?

➡ What do you think you need to do to tap into your core as a leader more completely and leverage your personality, ability, spirit, and thinking attributes more fully?

➡ What aspects, if any, of your core abilities should you dial up, dial back, or dial in?

CONCLUSION

Core Concept: The Fraud Factor is real. Feeling like a fraud is something that happens to nearly all of us as we approach situations and circumstances in our lives for which we do not feel fully prepared. When we find ourselves in the middle of such situations, we begin to listen to our own irrational fears and the lie that tell us why we are inadequate in that moment. As you have discovered, getting past The Fraud Factor can be difficult and complicated. In order to learn and grow, you must experience a bit of dissonance from the new or unusual circumstances you face, but not to the point where you become destabilized and question who you are at the core.

We have seen from the perspective, stories, examples, and discussion questions in this book that **The Fraud Factor** is real. Feeling like a fraud is something that happens to nearly all of us as we approach situations and circumstances in our lives for which we do not feel fully prepared. When we enter or find ourselves in the middle of such situations, we begin to listen to our own irrational fears and the lie that tell us why we are inadequate in that moment.

As you have discovered in this book, getting past **The Fraud Factor** has some complicated layers associated with it. In order to learn and grow, you must experience a bit of dissonance from new or unusual circumstances you face, but not to the point where you become destabilized. The paradox is that you usually need to shift your behaviors to accommodate to the dissonance of such new circumstances, yet, the changes you make must occur within the secure parameters of your core personality, abilities, and motivations. Otherwise, you experience destabilization, which can be overwhelming.

The mental shifts you make are what create the learning and subsequent growth. Failure to make those shifts leads to little or no growth—that is, you do not learn from it. Likewise, situations that require too large a shift will smother your potential growth in fear.

What needs to change in these situations is your thinking and the strategies you employ. In some conditions you face, everything you knew to be true and effective seems suddenly false and inadequate to the task. When that occurs, you might start to believe the Big, Fat Lie that you are inadequate at the core. This can lead to total destabilization and, in the end, failure that might conclude in the termination of your employment. As we discovered, frauds get fired.

The key is to recognize immediately when you feel the dissonance and find yourself believing the false narrative that everything you know is wrong—that you are inadequate to the task. Once you realize that the Big Fat Lie has crept in and has undermined your effectiveness, you can begin to counterbalance your reaction to the situation. How? As we described over several chapters in the book, by first making sure you are in the right fit, where you are clearly functioning in your sweet spot. Once you determine that this is true, you can begin to identify how you get in your own way. It is important to catch yourself before you get too far off the track.

You can remind yourself at this point who you are at the core as a person: your signature personality traits, abilities, and motivations. Doing this re-grounds you to what you bring to the table in the situation at hand. Sometimes, it helps at this point to involve others who know you well. Ask them to share their perspective on your core attributes that are needed in this particular circumstance. Reminding yourself who you are, identifying your genuine strengths and character attributes, and soliciting feedback from others is a critical step to counterbalancing your fraud feelings and behaviors.

The sad truth is that we all undermine ourselves by feeling like a fraud in specific situations in our lives. I have yet to meet anyone, out of the thousands I have helped as an executive coach and leadership development trainer, who is not negatively impacted by these fraudulent feelings at one time or another. However, I am confident that you will be able to take the insights in this book and apply them to your own life and work. The result will be you genuinely leading and interacting with others from your true self—the core of who you are!

AFTERWORD

An analogy from a completely different arena might help provide additional perspective for you on the importance of recognizing fraudulent feelings and the accompanying Big Fat Lie, and then interacting with others from your genuine core. Allow me to introduce you to Tim, a young man whom I met through an organization in my community. At the time we met, he was speaking to a group that included me as a participant.

Tim shared a powerful story from his life that is a metaphor for how the Fraud Factor develops in people like you and me. You see, Tim grew up confused about his gender identity, even though he was born with all the requisite male body parts and a masculine role-model for a father. One reason for his confusion was that, as he moved from late elementary school into middle and high school, his voice never grew lower like the other boys in his class. Instead, he spoke from a female-sounding high falsetto all the time.

Much like Tiny Tim, the entertainer who sang "Tiptoe Through The Tulips" in the 1970's, people around him began to question whether he was really a male. This young Tim brought laughter and derision upon himself from other males whenever he opened his mouth to speak in his high falsetto.

Because of this affectation in his voice, Tim began to feel like a fraud as a male. He became confused about his gender, and he began to believe the Big Fat Lie that he was not really masculine at all, and never would be. The names other boys called him on the school playground added to his confusion and began to convince him that he was homosexual. Since he had not found his voice as a genuine male, he embraced a more feminine attitude and stance. His voice did not deepen, and he became fully destabilized in his identity as a male.

Even when he went on to college, he continued to speak in a falsetto voice and struggle with his gender destabilization. Since nothing had ever changed, and he did not find his voice as a male, his parents, siblings, friends, and others simply assumed he would always speak in this voice. They conjectured that, perhaps, it was related to a very low testosterone level, damaged vocal chords, or some other medical reason.

One day, something rather miraculous occurred. Tim happened to meet Yvonne, a vocal coach who immediately noticed his odd voice, and began to ask him about it. Through her gentle questions, she discovered that he had never spoken in a normal, male range. She offered to help him figure out why he did not have a masculine voice.

Sitting at a piano with him in her studio office, Yvonne asked Tim to sing a range of notes to match those she played on the keys. She started on the higher keys at her right hand and worked him slowly and deliberately toward the lower keys at her left hand. He continued to match the notes she played, including those that were in the deep, male vocal range. Smiling, she turned to him and said, *"Well, we know now that your vocal chords can produce those masculine sounds. It seems like, for some reason, you have chosen not to use them."*

What Yvonne spoke was the truth, and it cut right through him in a powerful way. You see, Tim did have the voice he needed to be effective as a male in the world, but his self-doubts and confusion had stopped him from using that voice. Instead, he employed a false one (a falsetto) to mask the dissonance he felt. Eventually, that dissonance turned into destabilization.

Yvonne had literally helped him find his voice for the first time as an adult. When I met Tim, his voice was masculine, clear, and articulate. There was no evidence that his voice had ever been abnormally high, no indication that **The Fraud Factor** had previously undermined his masculine gender identity.

Like Tim, you can reconnect to your true voice as a person and begin to speak again from that foundation. Remember, the most effective you will ever be is when you lead from your genuine voice, the authentic core of who you are. This is the prescription for counteracting the feelings of being a fraud when they appear in your work and life.

GLOSSARY OF TERMS

360 degree feedback: online ratings and comments from a variety of perspectives that typically include manager, direct reports, peers, and others. The goal of this type of feedback is to find out how others who work with an individual view his or her performance on a set of core competencies. These competencies usually include ones related to building relationships, solving problems, and taking initiative. (See page 27)

Big Fat Lie: the belief that you are not adequate in the situation or circumstances you face, and that you must somehow change who you are at the core. (See page 42)

Core: the essence of who you are as a person, your fundamental nucleus of unique characteristics that are sustained, consistent, and enduring over time. Measurable core characteristics include personality, abilities, motivations, and beliefs/values. (See page 18)

Destabilization: a deep and lasting instability that undermines and overwhelms your ability to function with consistent actions and beliefs. It disrupts and weakens your capacity to fulfill your roles over time. (See page 16)

Dissonance: a temporary lack of consistency or compatibility between your actions and beliefs in a particular situation. It is a short-term instability that feels unpleasant and motivates you toward resolution. (See page 15)

Fraud: feeling inauthentic, like a phony or charlatan in a particular situation that, in your mind, requires you to act like someone very different from the person you really are. (See page 6)

Fraudulent behaviors: those things that you utilize to cover your fear and confusion, and to try to be what you think others want you to be. For most people, these kinds of behaviors are awkward and ill-fitting, and they are typically carried out in an ineffective manner. (See page 32)

Growth paradox. (See page 16)

- To **shift your approach** and show evidence of true growth, you must accommodate to new circumstances and demands by changing some of your core beliefs, which then shifts your behavior; however,
- To **sustain this growth**, you must stay within the boundaries of your core personality, abilities, and motivations. Otherwise, the changes will be brief and inauthentic.

ROI: a common set of initials in the business world, meaning 'return on investment'. (See page 80)

Sweet spot: psychologists call this the optimal level of arousal. Your sweet spot of alertness is the place where you function with the utmost confidence and competence. Here, you are the most motivated and alert, and the fraud factor has very little effect on your successful achievement of desired outcomes. Most people would agree that there is a level of alertness that leads to their best performance, whether in sports, artistic endeavors, public speaking, or facilitating a team discussion. (See page 68)

ABOUT THE AUTHOR

ruce E. Roselle, PhD is a psychologist, author, speaker, and executive coach. He brings a breadth of experience and a deep sense of purpose to the task of aiding leaders to become as effective as they can be. For more than 25 years, Bruce has served a variety of for-profit, non-profit, public, and governmental organizations, helping them select and develop the best talent.

A recognized expert in the field of leadership development, Bruce has been a frequent speaker at professional conferences and corporate events, and his views on leadership topics have appeared in newspapers, journals, magazines, radio, television, and Internet blogs and postings.

More importantly, Bruce is a committed Christian whose faith infuses his work every day. Because he believes deeply in the scriptural encouragement to *"do your work as if doing it for God,"* this perspective drives his integrity and relationship focus with clients. He understands that the feeling of being a fraud does not come from God; rather, it creeps in from other forces inside and outside of each person.

He recognizes that the process of getting real again must be grounded on knowing who we are from God's perspective—how we were gifted, talented, nurtured, and blessed from birth on.

Bruce's ongoing prayer in his work over the years has been to have the wisdom, compassion, discernment, courage, and patience it takes to help others develop into the leaders they were destined to be. The most powerfully effective any person will ever be happens when that person genuinely expresses the personality, abilities, spirit, and thinking that God intended for him or her.

His first book, **Vital Truths** (2002) outlines seven ways that people can recharge their batteries and rekindle energy, joy, and enthusiasm in their lives. It reflects the many ways in which external circumstances sap one's motivation and optimism, and it includes the wisdom of various 'wholehearted leaders' who manage to stay upbeat and positive despite the circumstances around them.

Four years later, his second book, **Fearless Leadership** (2006), captured the essence of how leaders' irrational fears, faulty beliefs, and anchor lies undermine their capacity to function at their high performance best. Using the stories of 40 actual coaching clients, this book describes reactions versus responses to stressful circumstances, identifies catalyst situations and early warning signs, and provides a seven-step process for getting past fearful reactions in order to break through to leading fearlessly™. This book won two awards (Best Self-Help, silver; Best Business, bronze) from independent publishing organizations.

In many ways, **The Fraud Factor** is the prequel to **Fearless Leadership**, though it was written 10 years later. That is, this latter book outlines why we feel like frauds in the first place, how we must look at our actual work to determine if it is the right fit, who we are at the core, how we learn and grow through circumstances, and how we can break loose from our internal fears and lies to get real again. The two books together form a powerful and truthful set of tools to look at why we as human beings get in our own way, what to do to recognize the problem, and how to work through it to be genuinely who we are in our daily interactions with others.

It is Bruce's heartfelt desire that **The Fraud Factor** enable its readers (you) to go forth genuinely and fearlessly, so that you can be fruitful to the greatest degree in your work and life. You can do this!

OTHER BOOKS BY BRUCE E. ROSELLE, PHD

Vital Truths: the secret to living and leading wholeheartedly (2002)
Beaver's Pond Press, Edina, MN

Designed to help leaders at all levels in organizations live and lead wholeheartedly, Vital Truths describes this as a lifelong commitment to continuously shape your attitude, heart, and will. It outlines a learning process that will lead to greater joy and fulfillment in a person's work and life. Specifically, this book highlights the stories of many individuals who work and live wholeheartedly by following these seven vital truths:

- Know the purpose in what you propose to do
- Generate enthusiasm to achieve great things
- Focus on the beauty that still remains
- Find hope in the thought that things will get better
- Think less about yourself and more about others
- Jog yourself physically, psychologically, spiritually
- Accept what you cannot change, change what you can

Fearless Leadership: conquering your fears and the lies that drive them (2006) Leader Press: Minneapolis, MN

Dedicated to helping leaders at all levels in all organizations become more effective, this book highlights the difference between reacting and responding to situations. What gets in the way of thoughtful responses? Underlying irrational fears and unconscious faulty beliefs. This book outlines seven steps to help leaders and others recognize when their buttons are pushed, so they can, instead, respond in a high performance manner:

1. Identify catalyst situations that often push your buttons
2. Be alert for 'early warning' signs that you are beginning to react
3. Ask yourself the question, *"What is causing me to react irrationally here?"*
4. Get further perspective on the situation by asking yourself, "How big a deal is this?"
5. Reinforce your healthy beliefs about leading others, interacting with them
6. Establish the bedrock truth about yourself
7. Act on the truth of your new perspective